Revolutionary Ceramics

Soviet Porcelain 1917–1927

Nina Lobanov-Rostovsky

REVOLUTIONARYCERAMICS

Soviet Porcelain 1917-1927

STUDIO
VISTA

Cassell
Artillery House, Artillery Row
London SE1P 1RT

British Library Cataloguing in Publication Data
Lobanov-Rostovsky, Nina
Revolutionary ceramics: Soviet porcelain 1917–1927
1. Soviet porcelain, history
I. Title
738.20947

ISBN 0–289–80031–5

Designed by Mikhail Anikst
Typeset by Wyvern Typesetting Ltd, Bristol
Printed and bound in Singapore by Toppan Ltd.

Acknowledgements

In memory of my father,
Guillaume Georges-Picot

I am indebted to many people for assistance in the preparation of this book. Some were inspirational, others provided specific help. Foremost in both areas was Nicholas Lynn, collector and connoisseur of Russian porcelain of all periods. At a time when no Western museum had even started thinking about acquiring representative pieces of the most dynamic period of twentieth-century ceramic design, he was putting together a collection which now represents a chapter in the history of Russian revolutionary art. Intellectual encouragement came from the books, articles and letters of Dr. John E. Bowlt. Dr. Bowlt is a model of open-handed scholarship with his information, advice and prompt help. Alexis de Tiesenhausen of Christie's, London, was always a generous source of information, encouragement and help, as was Dr. Irmela Franzke at the Badisches Landesmuseum, Karlsruhe and Natalya Sergeevna Petrova, Curator at the Lomonosov Pocelain Factory Museum, Leningrad. To Olga Iosifovna Rybakova of Leningrad I owe special thanks for several interesting visits, much unpublished information and many photographs, as well as warm hospitality.

I also wish to make acknowledgement to the Wolfson Foundation of Decorative and Propaganda Arts for permitting me to reprint much of my article 'Soviet Propaganda Porcelain' which first appeared in the *Journal of Decorative and Propaganda Arts*, no. 11, winter 1989.

Grateful thanks to Countess N. Sumarokov-Elston, Rosanna Kelly and Marussia Mirchevska for their helpful translations from Russian texts, and to Jane Vaughan for proofreading the foreword.

My thanks also go to the following people, who either obtained pictures and books for me, or made pertinent suggestions, and to the keepers and the institutions and museums which they represent:

In the Soviet Union – E. A. Ivanova, Curator for Decorative Arts at the State Russian Museum in Leningrad; T. N. Novosir, Porcelain Collection at the Museum-Palace of Petrodvorets; E. S. Eritzian, Director of the State Ceramics Museum at Kuskovo; Academician D. S. Likhachev, Chairman of the Cultural Foundation, U.S.S.R.; A. A. Sazonov, Cultural Foundation, Leningrad; also in Leningrad, M. Guerman, A. S. Shuster, B. N. Vasiliev and Mrs. N. Altman. In Moscow, L. V. Andreeva; B. I. Brodsky; Lady Braithwaite at the British Embassy; Y. M. Ovsyannikov; Professor D. V. Sarabianov; the late Professor I. S. Zhilbershtein, T. Rubinshtein; V. Stepanov at 'Rodina', and Nicholas Louis.

In London – Laurence Kelly; L. Krassina Mathias; Ivor Mazure; Anita Besson; Mrs. W. Raeburn; A. Flegon; Asya Chorley at Sotheby's; Angela, Gräfin von Wallwitz; Sir Peter and Lady Wakefield; Jan Peter Bethge; Stephen Saunders; Tatiana Wolff, Annely Juda and Salim Nassar.

In Hull, Martyn Chalk; in Oxford, David Elliott; and in Scotland, Fiona Burnett. In Brussels, Baroness Guy de Wouters d'Oplinter; in Geneva, Gerda Bouvier; in Paris, Mr. and Mrs. J. Lempert; in Germany, Vasilii Rakitin; and in Greece, George Varsos. In New York, Eva Zeisel, Robert Coates at MOMA and A. Rabinovich; in Connecticut, Thomas P. Whitney; in Texas, Schatzie Lee; and in Wisconsin, L. and H. Shapiro.

Other owners of fine private collections in England, Moscow and Leningrad preferred to remain nameless. I thank them for their hospitality and trust and for allowing me to see and to handle their plates and figurines.

At John Calmann and King, I owe thanks to my publisher, Laurence King, to my omniscient editor, Sophie Collins, and to Mikhail Anikst, graphic designer extraordinary, who had the idea of turning my catalogue of the Nicholas Lynn collection into a book.

Finally, heartfelt thanks to my husband Nikita. It is due to his intense belief in *ars longa vita brevis* that we have wonderful friends in the Soviet Union and know the Moscow and Leningrad museum and art world intimately. Without him this book would not exist.

Nina Lobanov-Rostovsky
August, 1989

Contents

Plates

Agit Pieces

During the first years of Communism, porcelain was used as a means of disseminating propaganda and plates were painted with slogans.

Symbolic and Commemorative Pieces

This category includes plates which, though free of slogans, fall within the definition of agitprop because of the message they project about the value of work. They show the symbols and monograms of the new republic and commemorate festivals and anniversaries.

Figurines

These represent characters from the new Soviet epoch as well as typically Russian figures.

Traditional themes
These represent scenes and subjects of eternal Russia – rural life, motherhood, peasants and fishermen.
104

Russian Folklore
Subjects drawn from folklore – the Firebird, Sadko, wood spirits and scenes from the tales of Pushkin.
120

The Avant Garde
Cubist, Suprematist and abstract pieces.
126

Foreword

My collection of Soviet porcelain was born – by proxy – shortly after dawn one Friday morning in 1967 at the open-air Bermondsey Market south of London Bridge. Appropriately, the year marked the fiftieth anniversary of the October Revolution.

A stall holder unpacked five unusual plates which instantly created a flurry of excitement as they emerged from their newspaper wrappings. Did anyone present realize that this effect was precisely what the plates had been created to achieve in the first place?

Painted in vibrant colours and decorated with slogans, hammers, sickles and symbols of the Revolution, the plates stood out in the market clutter. They caught the eye of a collector, James Blewitt of Boxted Hall, Essex, who asked the price (it was £7 each) and without hesitation said, 'I'll have them all.' You had to act quickly in those days, because there was always another collector ready to pounce.

Indeed, someone did exclaim, 'But I saw them first! Please let me have just one.' Nothing doing. Blewitt prevailed, and the nucleus of what was later to become my collection was formed.

Over the next ten years, Blewitt bought every Soviet plate he came across in the markets and in London shops. They had little to do with his vast collection of English commemorative ceramics, but he was fascinated by the curious plates and could not resist buying them.

In the meantime I had moved from New York to London and, with my partner, Jan Peter Bethge, had launched, first, a small but thriving antiques business in Portobello Road (the world's best proving-ground for budding dealers and collectors) and, later, a small shop called 'Hope & Glory' in Kensington Church Street. Because we specialized in commemorative pots, James Blewitt became a client, soon a good friend and always an inspiration, because he is a true collector, in every sense of the word. His enormous collection was a source of endless fascination. I spent many happy hours sifting through stacks of plates of all descriptions, commemorating a multitude of events. Then, on a weekend visit, I came across several piles of the Soviet plates, which included the first 'Bermondsey Five' and about two dozen subsequent additions.

My first reaction to the plates was much the same as Blewitt's a decade earlier. Although I had only a vague idea of what I was looking at and what they represented, I knew at once that they were exciting, and that I wanted to own them. Also, they were 'Russian' (albeit Soviet), and my business – and my passion – had already begun to turn towards Russian works of art. Indeed, 'Hope & Glory' was becoming more Russian and less British every day. In 1982 we moved to 69 Kensington Church Street, where the present shop, 'The Winter Palace', is wholly devoted to Russian art, mainly pre-1917.

I gradually persuaded James to part with the Soviet plates stacked on his floor, and my search for more led me all over Europe and America. The prices began to rise, but so did my enthusiasm, as well as that of my partner, Jan. I learned that each piece had its own history and that the artists who had painted them had names, sometimes important ones.

In short, the collection grew steadily (it now consists of about 250 pieces), and the whole story and study began to emerge. The result is this book by Nina Lobanov-Rostovsky.

It was, in fact, Nina's husband, Nikita (also a keen collector), who uttered a truism about collecting which I have kept firmly in mind over the years, especially when I am forced to sacrifice in order to obtain yet another plate, figurine or cup and saucer: 'To have a great collection it's got to hurt.'

Well, the 'hurt' has certainly manifested itself many times. The joy, however, is always there . . . with an almost revolutionary fervour.

Nicholas Lynn
London, May 1989

Author's Note

This book on Soviet propaganda porcelain does not pretend to be an exhaustive account of the subject. It has grown out of the cataloguing of one superb private collection. Much more research needs to be done in the rich sources of Soviet collections and archives, both public and private, and I hope that this study will be followed by broader and more detailed investigations. My intention was merely to identify the artists in the Nicholas Lynn collection, the sources from which they drew the subjects they painted on platters, plates, teapots, cups and saucers, and the various factory marks and artists' signatures and marks found on the reverse of these pieces. Most of the examples of Suprematist porcelain were drawn from Soviet museums. A few specific notes follow, which the general reader should find helpful.

St. Petersburg, Petrograd, Leningrad

The city of St. Petersburg underwent a series of name changes. Until the outbreak of the First World War it was known by a semi-German name: Sankt Peterburg. In 1914 the name was Russified to Petrograd, which was in use for ten years until Lenin's death in 1924, when the city was renamed Leningrad. All the names are used in the book as appropriate to the period under discussion.

The Imperial/State/Porcelain Factory

The Imperial Porcelain Factory in Leningrad was founded in the mid eighteenth century. After the February Revolution in 1917 it was renamed the State Porcelain Factory, and in 1925 it became the Lomonosov Porcelain Factory. Again, all three names are used in this book as appropriate to the period under discussion.

Dates

In the late sixteenth century most of Europe adopted the Gregorian or New Style calendar. Russia, however, retained the Julian or Old Style calendar. By the twentieth century, Old Style dates lagged thirteen days behind New Style. On 14 February 1918 the Soviet Government decreed that henceforth all dates were to be in conformity with the Gregorian calendar. This means that although the Revolution continues to be known as the October Revolution, its anniversary is celebrated on what is now 7 November. The dates given in the text, captions and biographies prior to February 1918 are Old Style.

Transliteration

The transliteration system used is a modified version of the Library of Congress system; the soft and hard signs have been rendered by 'i' or omitted (for example, Vasilievich). When a Russian name has a widely used transliteration that varies from the above system (for example, Alexandre Benois, not Aleksandr Benua), this has been used. In the case of certain names, a spelling given is that adopted by the artists themselves when they emigrated (for example, Chekhonin/Tchekhonine). Spellings may vary in bibliographical references according to the language in which a text is written.

Revolutionary Ceramics

Soviet Porcelain 1917–1927

The aftermath of the Russian Revolution destroyed many traditions and millions of lives, but it did not destroy porcelain. Instead the revolutionaries were ordered by Lenin and Lunacharsky to use the stocks of white blanks they found in the Imperial Porcelain Factory in Petrograd as a propaganda tool. The style of decoration varied widely, from pieces disseminating straightforward Marxist slogans, accompanied by symbols of the new republic, to designs retaining the influences of classicism, of ikons, and of Russian peasant and folklore traditions. This porcelain has become an art document of the epoch.

Revolution and Propaganda Propaganda was of crucial importance to the Bolshevik government,[1] whose hold over Russia was precarious at best in the years immediately after the October 1917 Revolution. When Lenin made a separate peace with Germany early in 1918, the treaty of Brest-Litovsk required the surrender of one-quarter of Russia's territory, one-third of her population and croplands, and more than half of her industries.[2] Civil war was raging. Opposition flared up on every side. Counter-revolutionary forces, known as the 'Whites' and led by generals from the Imperial Army, quickly won control in the south. At the same time, Russia's erstwhile allies, France, Britain and the United States, sent troops into the country – at first to force it back into the war and then to aid the Whites. The Japanese landed in Vladivostock. Thus, from October 1917 to the spring of 1921, the Bolsheviks struggled desperately to maintain power. Their survival depended largely on the new Red Army, which Trotsky was in the process of building into an efficient, loyal fighting force. Compulsory military service was introduced for the working class. Trotsky ranged the country in an armoured train, seldom staying more than a day in any one place. Simultaneously a campaign of agitation and propaganda (agitprop) was launched. This was directed towards reconciling the populace, both literate and illiterate, to the new government and the socialist way of life.

Anatolii Lunacharsky, the head of the People's Commissariat for Public Enlightenment (Narkompros), which was responsible for the administration of education and the arts, quickly set about enlisting the help of artists in the battle for hearts and minds. Lunacharsky was both a member of the Bolshevik inner circle and a highly cultivated man who had had travelled widely. He had access to Lenin and was able to defend both artistic projects and the artists themselves when necessary.

The artists were urged to leave their easels and to design decorations for street pageants praising the Revolution, and for the First of May and the October Revolution anniversary celebrations. They were to decorate agitprop trains, ships and trucks. At first these trains were sent to the various war fronts filled with political literature, news from the capital and presents for wounded soldiers. Later, agitprop trains, ships and trucks, gaily painted with revolutionary messages and filled with trained agitators and representatives from the various commissariats were systematically sent all over the country. At this time, in pre-radio days, such propaganda was astonishingly effective. Each train was equipped with a small library, a bookshop, a printing press for producing pamphlets, a gramophone for broadcasting Lenin's speeches, and a coach fitted out for meetings and for showing short propaganda films. In rural areas most of the peasants, mainly illiterate, had never seen a film before and they were fascinated. Some of the films were aimed specifically at them, describing more efficient agricultural methods, urging them to learn how to read and write, and encouraging them to be inoculated against disease.

Never before had artists and writers been so closely linked with the politics of their country. They took themselves very seriously and, like the political authorities, issued orders and decrees. The new republic became a canvas and a stage for artists of various political beliefs. Vast rallies were held at which poets read their verse praising the Revolution and ridiculing its enemies. Rows of houses were painted with enormous murals or covered with posters, relating the latest events in an eye-catching and often satirical form.

In April 1918 Lenin announced a plan of 'monumental propaganda'. His idea was to have erected, in towns and villages throughout the country, statues and memorial plaques designed to inspire the people with the events and achievements of the Revolution. He explained, first to Lunacharsky and then to Trotsky that he was:

> anxious to have as many revolutionary monuments erected as possible, even if they were of the simplest sort, like busts or memorial tablets, to be placed in all the towns, and, if it could be managed, in the villages as well, so that what had happened might be fired into the people's imagination, and leave the deepest possible furrow in the popular memory.[3]

Most of the statues, representing figures as diverse as Marx, Gogol, Garibaldi and Robespierre, were executed in plaster, or in cement of such poor quality that they crumbled upon being erected, or were washed away by the first rain.[4] Several were later remade in stone or in bronze.

A more successful form of agitational art was the Russian Telegraph Agency (ROSTA) window. Political posters and wall newspapers had become substitutes for newspapers throughout war-torn Russia. However, wall newspapers were usually posted in the corridors of institutional buildings and thus were not accessible to everyone, whereas signs and posters in store windows could be seen by all passers-by, and were also safe from wind, rain and graffiti. So, in 1919, the artist Mikhail Cheremnykh devised a new wall newspaper for ROSTA. It consisted of the usual bulletin conveying the latest news in telegraphic style, but illustrated with cartoons or satirical sketches which were hand painted or stencilled. These bulletins were mounted on a board that would fit into an ordinary store window. Vladimir Mayakovsky, Dimitri Moor, Konstantin Vialov and other outstanding artists soon joined Cheremnykh in producing ROSTA windows, which were changed at least weekly and sometimes more frequently. It is within this context of the arts and crafts dedicated to propagandizing the achievements of the Bolshevik Revolution that we must study the output of the State Porcelain Factory.

The State Porcelain Factory   Porcelain and politics have been linked historically in Russia and elsewhere. For instance, the Russo-Turkish wars of the eighteenth century had been commemorated in a few figures made by the Imperial Porcelain Factory. Portraits of the heroes of battles in the 1812 war againt Napoleon (Kutuzov, Bagration, Platov and others) appeared on vases, plates and cups made in various Russian factories of the early nineteenth century. In France, political events and feelings were also recorded on ceramics during the French Revolution. Small factories in Nevers and elsewhere created revolutionary plates decorated with civic maxims and symbols of the

Revolution, such as tricolour ribbons, a red Phrygian bonnet topping a sword or tree, or a cock perched on a cannon, crowing 'I sing to Liberty'. Later, figurines were produced representing the victorious generals: Joubert, Marceau, Hoche and, of course, Napoleon.

However, it was the Soviet leaders, soon after the October Revolution of 1917, who had the idea of using porcelain as a systematic means of propaganda both within the Soviet Union and abroad.

The Imperial Porcelain Factory, located on what is now the Obukhovskoy Oborony Prospekt on the southern outskirts of Leningrad, was founded in the first half of the eighteenth century and worked exclusively for the Imperial court, to which it supplied dinner services, articles for the adornment of palaces and yachts, replacement plates for the existing services, and presentation services, vases, figurines and other works of art to be given as presents by the Imperial household. During the First World War the factory worked for the Imperial army and army hospitals. Many of its workers went to war, leaving behind only a skeleton workforce. After the February Revolution of 1917 it was renamed the State Porcelain Factory. Still later, in 1925, it became the Lomonosov Porcelain Factory, as a tribute to Mikhail Vasilievich Lomonosov (1711–65), Russia's first great scientist. This is still its name today (the abbreviations 'IPF,' 'SPF' and 'LPF' have been used as appropriate in the captions).

After the February and October Revolutions the artistic administration of the country represented a picture of extreme confusion and, at times, anarchy. The Bolsheviks had given relatively little thought to the way in which they would administer the country after taking over. Immediately after the October Revolution many pragmatic decisions had to be taken in education, art and industry. There was no overall set pattern of administration. In many cases specialists were able to keep the jobs they had held before the Revolution. This was the case at the Imperial Porcelain Factory, where the reorganization took place fairly swiftly and smoothly. After the February Revolution it had come under the aegis of the Ministry of Trade and Industry of the new regime, which took absolutely no notice of it. Everyone at the factory stayed on, and in theory it was ruled by a workers' control commission. Artists and sculptors ranked as workers, so there was no 'class' problem. The sculpture workshop, headed by Vasilii Kuznetsov, and the painting workshop, headed by Rudolf Vilde, continued working on pre-revolutionary models. (This is why one sometimes finds such items with post-Revolution factory marks and dates on them.) Both of these workshops were soon threatened with closure, however, because there was no outlet for decorative wares.

Meetings were held and a petition presented to the Ministry, but with no concrete result. After the October Revolution the factory came briefly under the jurisdiction of the Commissariat of Agriculture; a few months later, by a decision of the Council of People's Commissars of 23 March 1918,[5] it was placed under the authority of Narkompros.

The transfer of the factory to the jurisdiction of Narkompros was due chiefly to the efforts of two men. The first, Sergei Chekhonin, was a specialist consultant, first to the Ministry, then to the Commissariat of Agriculture, before, during and after the Revolution. His areas of specialization within the wide-ranging department were artistic crafts and craft schools, and everything that concerned them. After the October Revolution Chekhonin organized a special art council comprising some of the most influential names in Russian art to discuss the problems and goals of the artistic industries. A general meeting of the council was called, to be attended by all members, and the workers' commission. Lunacharsky attended it with Shterenberg, the head of the fine art department of Narkompros,[6] and approved everything that was suggested.

The other energetic reformer was Piotr Vaulin, who took upon himself the task of the general reorganization of the factory. He was well qualified to do this, having run, first, the Abramtsevo Ceramic Studio in Moscow and then his own ceramic factory at Kikerino, near St. Petersburg, before the Revolution. (Both Chekhonin and Alexander Matveev had worked at his factory.) In January 1918, in a proposal submitted to Lunacharsky, Vaulin outlined plans and targets for the 'new' factory, suggesting that it should be raised scientifically and technically to at least the same level as similar factories in other countries. He recommended that its aims be to help the development of the ceramic and glass industries in Russia, to search for new methods of production in these industries, and to raise the artistic standards from the rather insipid level they had sunk to before the Revolution, initiating the production of items that would embody revolutionary ideals. The proposal covered all aspects of the factory's possible future activity very thoroughly. Impressed by the plan's conciseness and originality, Lunacharsky asked Vaulin to become one of the factory's directors when it was transferred to Narkompros.

The transfer encountered, at first, some opposition from the workers' commission at the factory. However, Lunacharsky managed to reassure the workers' deputies that their future was secure, telling them that Narkompros intended the factory to become 'a great world centre for the scientific study of porcelain'.[7]

At the first meeting of the management Chekhonin was elected to the post of artistic director. Superbly trained and experienced in the fields of tile murals and ceramics, enamel, graphic design, miniatures and gilding, Chekhonin experienced no difficulty in bridging the two worlds of painting and ceramics. Although he is sometimes accused of having 'sold out' artistically to the Revolution,[8] close study of his work reveals that this was not so. Chekhonin's firm commitment to artistic innovation was neither increased nor decreased by the consequences of the Revolution. Unlike Mayakovsky, he did not need the Revolution to give him a sense of direction – he was inspired not so much by revolutionary ideology as by purely artistic interest in the possibilities of new designs.

Vaulin, Chekhonin and Shterenberg were in charge of the general direction of the factory. P. Fricken became a director and took care of administrative and economic matters. Chekhonin held artistic control and Shterenberg liaised with IZO, the fine art department of Narkompros. All four worked in close collaboration with the workers' commission.[9] There were twelve workers in the painting section and 100 workers in all at the factory. The artists were required to familiarize themselves with the work previously done by artisans in order to acquire the habit of using a brush and bright colours on porcelain with ease. Chekhonin recruited many additional artists, both famous and unknown, to the art department of the factory. Among them were Mikhail Adamovich, Vasilii Timorev, Varvara Freze, Yelizaveta Rozendorf, Elena Danko, Maria Ivashintsova, Elizaveta Potapova, Alexandra Shchekotikhina-Pototskaya and Ekaterina Yakimovskaya in 1918; Ekaterina Bolsheva, Liubov Gaush, Alisa Golenkina, Maria Kirilova, Maria Lebedeva, Varvara Rukavishnikova and others in 1919 and Bazilka Radonich and others in 1920. (Zinaida Kobyletskaya, who had worked at the Imperial Porcelain Factory between 1912 and 1914, rejoined in 1918.)

Established artists such as Natan Altman, Veniamin Belkin, Mstislav Dobujinsky, Vladimir Lebedev, Vasilii Kandinsky and Valentin Sherbakov created designs for the State Porcelain Factory, although with the exception of Dobujinsky none of these artists even knew how to paint on porcelain.

For many of these painters, working at the factory was their first professional experience. Provided that they had been well trained, their inexperience did not worry the directors, who were attempting to create a porcelain 'nursery' for the new state. They banked on the lofty ideals and the excitement of the Revolution to inspire the artists' creative powers. Under Chekhonin's guidance many of the characteristic designs of elegantly worked slogans and inscriptions, monograms and dates, emblems, garlands and flowery borders were developed. He adapted his mastery of graphic art to porcelain and transferred the vignettes he loved to plates, cups and saucers. (His style of calligraphy is still used today on commemorative porcelain produced by the Lomonosov Porcelain Factory.)

Because the factory could not be reached by public transport, and there were no living quarters for the artists nearby, Chekhonin decided to relocate the artistic workroom in the centre of Petrograd. He found the ideal workshop in the building which, before the Revolution, had been the Baron A. Stieglitz Central School of Technical Design. Between 1918 and 1920 all design and original painting work took place here, but copying continued to be done at the factory itself. The artists worked at two long tables in a room that was often freezing – there was not always fuel for the Franklin stove, which, even when burning, could not heat the vast room properly. Frequently the artists had to work with their coats and mittens on. However, they later remembered it as an exciting and exhilarating time, despite the hardships and the food and fuel shortages, and they managed to express some of this excitement in their work. They were aware that they were part of an important propaganda campaign and that their art had a valued place in Soviet life.

Traditional Sources Before exploring the contemporary, revolutionary sources of inspiration for propaganda porcelain we should look at some earlier sources. Although propaganda porcelain was essentially born of the October Revolution, it had several grandparents. One was the *lubok*, or illustrated broadside, which had existed in Russia from the early seventeenth century. The lubok combined illustrations with text, and its subjects included religion and politics, as well as social problems and issues such as drunkenness, poverty and the position of women. It had a formative influence on the many artists of various backgrounds and schools who worked for the State Porcelain Factory immediately after the Revolution.

Another influence was the thousand-year-old tradition of Russian ikon painting, going back to the conversion of Kievian Russia to Christianity in 988. The word 'ikon' means image or likeness, in the sense of a visible and material reflection of things unseen or spiritual. Ikons not only are objects of worship in the Orthodox Church but are painted to be 'read' by the onlooker as pictorial commentaries on the Scriptures. The influence of ikons on both Chekhonin and Shchekotikhina-Pototskaya can be seen in their plates, 'Famine' and 'Motherhood' (shown in figs. 21 and 135). Furthermore, themes taken from ikons were often used, in altered form, on porcelain. For instance, St. George slaying the dragon (the triumph of Christianity over paganism) is often transformed into a Red Army soldier, on horse

Ivan Bilibin and Alexandra Shchekotikhina-Pototskaya.

Natalya Danko working in the sculpture workshop of the Lomonosov Porcelain Factory in the late 1920s.

Nikolai Suetin, Kazimir Malevich and Ilia Chashnik, left to right, circa 1923.

Sergei Chekhonin, self-portrait, 1921.

Elena Danko, Leningrad, 1935.

or on foot, slaying a dragon (the Revolution conquering either the bourgeoisie or the counter-revolution).

A third and very powerful forebear was the tradition of graphic design in newspapers and journals, including satirical cartoons. Satirical journals were published in Russia from the mid-nineteenth century onwards, and at first they were derivative of the West European journals of the period. However, during the two years following the Czar's October Manifesto of 1905,[10] establishing a limited freedom of the press, several hundred satirical journals were published. (It is difficult to establish the exact number because of continual name changes as they were closed down or severely fined.)

Between 1905 and 1907 satirical journals were very open and mordant in their criticisms of the government and the established institutions, and of the gap between liberal proclamations and the reality of bloody repression. During these two years – a period of great revolutionary enthusiasm followed by cruel czarist reaction – many members of the World of Art[11] group became active contributors to satirical magazines. Forgetful of their group's appeal for pure art, they created angry caricatures and satirical drawings denouncing the oppressors: the Czar, his generals and ministers. This period was highly educational for many artists, promoting the development of democratic feelings and a civic consciousness as well as an awareness of the importance and social significance of artistic endeavour. Chekhonin himself contributed to satirical journals and years later, after the October 1917 Revolution, when he designed his 'Signature Platter', on which were depicted the facsimile signatures of those he called the 'Activists of the Revolution', the names show that he favoured those who had been active pamphleteerists and contributors to satirical journalists, rather than theoreticians and organizers of men. Stalin's signature is conspicuously absent, as is that of Bukharin.

The Role of Porcelain   One of the problems faced by the Bolshevik government in its propaganda campaign was a shortage of materials. This problem did not exist initially at the State Porcelain Factory, which the new management found full of unpainted plates, ready to be covered with slogans and revolutionary themes. This was a legacy from the practice of producing a certain number of articles in advance: dinner services, platters, plates, jugs, teapots, cups and saucers, up to the 'biscuit', or unglazed, stage. These were stamped with the monogram of the reigning czar and the current year, then stored away until an order came through from the Imperial household for a service or for gifts for distinguished visitors. The required items would then be painted, glazed and fired.

Most of the blank porcelain found in the factory dated from the reign of the last czar, Nicholas II (1894–1917), but there was also a stock of blanks bearing the monograms of his father, Alexander III (1881–94) and his grandfather, Alexander II (1855–81), and a very few pieces that dated back to Nicholas I (1825–55). As each czar died, the leftover blanks stamped with his monogram had probably been pushed to the back of the storage shelves, where they gathered dust until the Revolution.

During the first two months after the overthrow of the Romanovs, artists at the porcelain factory had painted on pieces that had been marked simply with the date, 1917. These pieces are extremely rare. Between April and December 1917, pieces were marked with a crownless eagle in a hyphenated circle, and the date, 1917 – the symbol of the Provisional Government, designed by Ivan Bilibin. Between January and May 1918 the crownless eagle in a hyphenated circle continued to be used, but without a date.

After May 1918 the artists pragmatically started to use earlier monogrammed plates, but covered the Imperial mark with an oval or diamond-shaped patch of green or black paint and added the State Porcelain Factory mark of hammer, sickle and cog, designed by Alexis Eremeevich Karev, plus the year. From 1921 onwards, they usually left the Imperial monogram uncovered and simply added the State Porcelain Factory mark and the year alongside. Thus one usually finds both Soviet and Imperial marks on propaganda porcelain of the early years after the Soviet Revolution.

Slogans and Aphorisms Many of the wares produced by the State Porcelain Factory were inscribed with the slogans and aphorisms that were appearing in newspapers, on posters and on some of the newly erected monuments. Class struggle and the new revolutionary morality were important themes; another was the conflict between old and new. Extracts from speeches by or about Lenin provided a common source of inspiration, as did quotations from European socio-Utopian writers, revolutionary activists of many nationalities and the Communist Manifesto. However, sources were by no means limited to overtly political writings. Texts were also taken from classical authors such as Ovid and Cicero, from Dostoyevsky and Tolstoy, even from the Gospels. Some artists placed their hope in 'Labour, Science and Art' as a means of re-educating the social consciousness of the masses, and this is reflected in their designs and maxims. The range of source material was paralleled by an equally wide range in treatment; each artist had favourite motifs and a characteristic manner of execution.

In 1918 Chekhonin decorated a series of plates with slogans: 'He who is not with us is against us'; 'Struggle gives birth to heroes'; 'The mind cannot tolerate slavery'; 'What has been produced by working hands cannot be swallowed by a lazy belly'; and 'Science must serve the people' (see fig. 19). The stylized black letters circling the edge of the plate, interspersed with small, colourful flowers and leaves, are both powerful and appealing. Chekhonin, who was a consummate graphic artist, managed to make every inscription look elegant. His work was characterized by an attachment to the past, especially to the neo-classical style, as well as an enthusiasm for the present and the future, and for different trends in art. For example, his depiction of the hammer and sickle plus part of a cog, representing industry, shown in fig. 68, is surrounded by naïve field flowers and leaves recalling his attachment to folk art. This was followed by a plate known as 'Cubist design with hammer and sickle', shown in fig. 67. It is hard to believe that the same artist designed both plates.

The cautionary maxim 'He who does not work does not eat' is the message of the plate shown in fig. 2, which was designed by Mikhail Adamovich. This is an adaptation of St. Paul's Second Epistle to the Thessalonians, chapter 3, verse 10: 'If any will not work, neither let him eat.' It was incorporated into the Constitution of the RSFSR (Russian Soviet Federated Socialist Republic) in 1918. Here it dances around the border of the plate in multi-coloured letters, framing a composition that includes a portrait of Lenin (adapted from a famous portrait drawn from life by Natan Altman), some ration cards, half an Imperial eagle and a red star. In the prototype of this plate, created in 1921, the red star of the Revolution is on top of the eagle, obliterating and crushing it. However, when copies of the plate were ordered, the factory artists were obviously unfamiliar with the symbols and thought it a pity to cover up the eagle, so they painted the star underneath. One often finds such anomalies in agitprop porcelain.

Soviet heraldry acquired great importance in the decoration of art porcelain. An elegantly executed hammer and sickle on their own or entwined with flowers and foliage, or the initials RSFSR, elegantly calligraphed and adorned with flowers and gold, are often the only design elements on plates by Chekhonin and other artists. The Soviet art historian Lydia Andreeva explains the abundant use of gold on these plates by stating that, although it was associated with the Imperial regime and the luxurious past, it seemed appropriate for the emblems of the new republic – working tools – and its monogram, to be rendered in gold.[12]

The hammer and sickle are ingeniously employed in a plate entitled 'History of the Revolution, 1917' by Alexandra Shchekotikhina-Pototskaya (fig. 38). In addition to these emblems, the design includes yellow, blue and rust-red books with 'History [of the] Revolution 1917' written on them. Multi-coloured letters around the cavetto and the border read, 'To all who are young and brave at heart [put] into their hands a book, a sickle and a hammer', with the date, 1921. This is an adaptation of an old Russian saying, 'Into his hands a book', which people used to exclaim upon meeting a clever child. The Soviets have grafted a sickle and a hammer onto the older saying, thus rhyming *molod* (young) with *molot* (hammer).

Many Soviet propaganda plates have German inscriptions. There were various reasons for this. German was the language of Karl Marx and was spoken by many international revolutionaries. In addition, German inscriptions may have been aimed at the Baltic states, where German was the lingua franca. Also Lenin had hoped for a German revolution – a hope that faded after the failure of the November 1918 uprisings in Germany and the murders of the revolutionary heroes Karl Liebknecht and Rosa Luxemburg. However, German continued to be used in propaganda for a few years, perhaps because the unstable situation in Germany led the Soviet government to believe that the country would be susceptible to Communism.

Festive Themes   Some examples of agitprop porcelain are closely linked with the posters and the decor for revolutionary anniversaries and street festivities. Chekhonin designed various plates and platters with a red ribbon winding along the edges, intended to convey the atmosphere of festively decorated streets and fluttering banners. The motif decorating the banner that hung under the arch of the General Staff building in Petrograd for the first anniversary of the October Revolution was reproduced in a green and red plate, 'The land for the working people' by Natan Altman, shown in fig. 11. The green field incorporates a red rhombus containing a factory with tall stacks, a sickle and an ear of wheat, all painted in red, with the inscription, also in red, circling the edge. The monumental style of the design emphasizes the importance of the theme. Altman himself was responsible for the transformation of Palace Square for the anniversary celebrations. Several identical plates and a few drawings and descriptions by contemporary witnesses are all that remain as evidence of Altman's extraordinary decoration of Palace Square, the Winter Palace and the General Staff arch and building on the first anniversary of the October Revolution. Russia was on the verge of collapse, but Altman was allotted 50,000 feet of canvas to mount Futurist constructions and designs on the Winter Palace walls and on the General Staff arch. The Alexander column was also turned into a Futurist sculpture.

The celebration of the second anniversary of the October Revolution is the subject of several plates executed by Rudolf Vilde, an artist of the older generation, who, from 1906 until the mid-1930s, worked in the Imperial/State/Lomonosov Porcelain Factory, eventually becoming head of the painting workshop. Vilde's anniversary plates are always highly decorative. One, shown in fig. 48, has a cobalt-blue border decorated with leaves, flowers and tools, beautifully executed in etched gold and oxidized silver. The cavetto is decorated with a red banner inscribed in gold letters with 'Victory to the Workers' and '25 Oct.' Above the banner, also in gold, are the dates: 1917–19. When the oxidized silver blade of the sickle is rubbed clean the letters RSFSR appear. The plate both looks and feels like a plate manufactured by the Imperial Porcelain Factory, but it bears only the mark of the State Porcelain Factory. It would seem that some of the blanks manufactured under the czars escaped being monogrammed.

Numerous plates were designed to celebrate May Day, the workers' holiday, which had been banned under the czars. One such plate, shown in fig. 54, has a design by Vilde which consists of a bouquet incorporating pliers and a hammer, entwined with a red ribbon. At the top of the plate are the words 'In working we celebrate'. At the bottom is the date, 1 May 1920. Another plate by Vilde shows an open book in the cavetto with the slogan 'Knowledge lightens work' above it, and mechanic's tools, interspersed with colourful flowers and leaves circling the border (fig. 56).

The Old and New Although agitprop porcelain was focused emphatically on the present and the goals of modern Russia, many of its artists managed to incorporate themes and images from the past – reminders of Russia's distinctive traditions and identity.

A good example of this kind of work is a plate designed by Alisa Golenkina and shown in fig. 25. It is decorated with a torch-bearing man on a winged horse, flying over collapsing classical monuments, perhaps representing the past, which are in flames. Clouds of smoke are billowing upwards, but the winged horse and its rider are backed by golden rays. The border is circled in black letters proclaiming, in German, 'We shall set the world ablaze with the fire of the Third International'. A similar plate with the slogan in Russian can be seen at the Lenin State History Museum on Red Square. The horse and rider are Soviet adaptations of Ilia Muromets, the peasant's son on his flying horse. Although the old pagan religion had long since been vanquished by Christianity in Slavic countries, vestiges were still found in Russian epic poems. Among the most popular of these is the series devoted to Ilia Muromets, who, though a good Christian, is portrayed with a number of features apparently derived from the old pagan god of lightning, Perun.[13] Golenkina also seems to have been influenced by Ivan Bilibin's illustration of this subject, which was well known in Russia and appeared in the Berlin Russian journal *Jar Ptitza* (no. 8, 1922).

Another artist who explored this area – in her own porcelain painting and in designs that were executed by factory artists – was Alexandra Shchekotikhina-Pototskaya. Her trademarks are exuberant colours and subjects from Russian tradition and folklore: peasants feasting, bellringers, the sun and moon, motherhood, Snegurochka the Snowmaiden, fishermen and harmonica players.

Shchekotikhina came from a family of Old Believers, whose traditional crafts were ikon painting, book illumination and embroidery. She studied at art school under Roerich and Bilibin, and married the latter in the 1920s. Her studies and her trip through northern Russia, sponsored by her art school, deepened her love and knowledge of naïve, indigenous Russian art forms and were to influence her many fantastic compositions for porcelain. Her trip to Paris in 1913, at a time when Diaghilev's Russian Seasons were dazzling Parisians, deepened her awareness that there was much to be proud of in her 'barbaric' Russian heritage and its great vitality. Her familiarity with ikons encouraged her to disregard perspective, and her plates and cups and saucers are painted with all events occurring emphatically on the surface. There is no distance in Shchekotikhina's works. Contrast with gold leaf stresses the distinct quality of the joyous, enamelled colours employed, and despite the lack of pictorial structure, her designs are full of energy and impetuous rhythm with exaggerated figures and objects.

The collision between the old and the new is another theme found in agitprop porcelain, notably in the work of Maria Lebedeva. As an art student she toured northern Russian towns with Shchekotikhina, and she too absorbed the native art forms such as the lubok and was influenced by the bright colours of Russian peasant art. Symbolism and the fantastic are also characteristic of her plates. On an oval platter, shown in fig. 32, we have one of her most famous designs, 'The Telephonist'. He is a figure of the times, and he covers almost the entire platter. The edges are painted with a compact mass of colourful buildings, and the sky around the telephonist is filled with tangled telephone wires, golden aeroplanes and the barely discernible slogan, 'Peace to humanity building on the ruins of the past'. Another of her creations is the large dish shown in fig. 30, with the inscription 'I see plots everywhere of the rich seeking their own profit in the name, and under the pretext, of Good' – a paraphrase from Thomas More's *Utopia*. The dish is decorated with a huge red star, symbol of the new regime. The star's five points stretch out to the very edge of the dish, and the rim is painted with palaces alternating with factories (the old and the new). The factories are designed around the five points of the star, indicating perhaps that they are the support and the worker stronghold of the new regime. In the centre of the star is the head of a *tchekist*, or member of the secret police. The rays of the star contain a Red Army soldier, a Red sailor, a militia woman, a peasant woman and an unidentified genre figure. The aphorism is written in Lebedeva's usual spiky letters.

The Soviet People The people of Soviet Russia – the famous and the anonymous, the governing and the governed – are featured in many pieces of porcelain. Shchekotikhina's plate 'The Commissar' (fig. 36) shows a commissar crossing Uritsky Square (this was Palace Square before the Revolution, and is once more known as Palace Square today)[14] with the former General Staff headquarters in the background, and the Alexander column to one side. Iron-red letters circling the border spell out 'Uritsky Square, Petrograd 1921'. (The head of a government department in the Soviet Union was known as a commisssar until 1946, and was considered a worthy subject for the decoration of agitprop plates.)

The creator of the Red Army, Leon Trotsky, is depicted on a plate (fig. 5) by Mikhail Adamovich. His best plates are those celebrating the Red Army, in which he served from 1919 to 1921. (In a different vein, he designed a series of twelve plates decorated with architectural views of old St. Petersburg.)

The smiling, colourfully clad clown on the plate shown in fig. 81, which does not at first seem to be a propaganda piece at all, commemorates a famous pair of clowns, Bim and Bom, who, for a while, were granted permission by the Soviet authorities to satirize the shortcomings of the system, thus providing a safety valve for the harmless release of pent-up grievances against the regime. They were the subjects of posters, newspaper and magazine articles, and of many anecdotes.[15]

Dictators with secret police under their control can usually cope with conspiracy and rebellion, but a more insidious enemy is popular mockery. Court jesters have always been an outlet for this kind of problem. Peter the Great created his *Orden Shutov* ('merry counsellors') to allow certain designated individuals the right to speak the unthinkable, and Bim and Bom were the Soviet equivalents. The circus in which they performed was crowded night after night. Their jokes were the talk of Moscow – one person told them to another until the whole town knew the latest insults these two had uttered. Yet while they made fun of irritating restrictions and bureaucratic bungling, they never attacked the fundamental principles of Marxism. The government could rely on their never overstepping the limits of the permissible.

However, eventually the ruled outdid their rulers by turning the safety valve into a shield. People not only repeated the jokes; they added embellishments, expressing their own anger against the regime. They even devised their own malicious quips. According to one historian of the period,

> Anyone who wished to air a dangerous *mot*, now prefaced it with 'have you heard what Bim said yesterday?' and with this introduction anyone could with impunity give vent to the boldest contempt for the Soviets.[16]

A platter commemorating the work of Léon Bakst is shown in fig. 113. It is painted with his famous costume design for Nijinsky in the role of Iskander in the ballet *La Péri*. It was taken to Sweden by Alexandra Kollontai, who was a leading Bolshevik and an advocate of free love. She was a member of the Central Committee of the Bolshevik Party and became People's Commissar for Social Welfare after the Revolution. She also became the first Soviet woman ambassador – indeed the first woman ambassador in modern times – and, after brief postings to Norway and Mexico, was sent to Sweden (1930–1945) where she was very popular. She liked propaganda porcelain and took several fine pieces with her to Sweden as gifts for government officials and friends. This piece surfaced at a Stockholm auction in the spring of 1988. Its original price tag is still attached: 47.70 roubles. (Kollontai's signature appears among those of other important political activists on Chekhonin's 'Signature Platter'.)

The suffering of the Russian people in the famine and typhus epidemic of 1920–1921, which claimed millions of lives, provided tragic subject matter for the porcelain artists. A series of plates and dishes were made for a special sale to raise money for the starving population of the Volga region. These items were marked on the reverse with a special gold mark designed by Chekhonin and painted by hand. It consisted of the State Porcelain Factory mark, the date, 1921, and 'to benefit the starving', all in gold. There are apparently twenty-three items with this mark. The auction never took place, and they remained at the factory, but later some were sold. Three pieces are at the State Museum of Ceramics at Kuskovo.[17] According to Andreeva, 'This was the last agitational work to be made by different artists working on one particular subject; these dishes were designed by, amongst others, Chekhonin, Shchekotikhina-Pototskaya, Vilde and Kulikova.'[18]

Vilde painted the most striking of the famine plates, shown in fig. 55. It is also one of his most dynamic works. A worker holding a sledgehammer in his raised right hand and a rifle in his left is attacking a gloating death figure (the Great Reaper) who holds a scythe and carries away a sheaf of golden wheat. Golden Cyrillic letters circling the border read, 'In aid of the famine-stricken population of the Volga Region'. Chekhonin painted perhaps the most poignant of all the famine sale dishes, a grieving mother/madonna figure holding two starving, wailing children (fig. 21). They all have pale-green, skull-like faces. Chekhonin considered this to be one of his masterpieces, and managed to take it with him when he emigrated to Paris in 1928.

Figurines During the eighteenth and nineteenth centuries the Imperial Porcelain Factory had produced several series of figurines, including one called 'The Peoples of Russia'. It also produced numerous individual figurines in Rococo, Empire and other styles, of elegant ladies and gentlemen in period dress. All were superbly executed, but are, on the whole, rather insipid.

A more robust style emerged in other factories. In 1818 the Gardner Factory, on the outskirts of Moscow, began to produce a series of porcelain figures based on engravings from the St. Petersburg magazine, *The Magic Lantern*. They represented artisans and tradesmen from the streets of the capital. These figurines were very popular and were eventually reproduced by most of the other factories. Russian porcelain figurines produced by the private workshops and factories were usually full of popular humour and biting satire against the landowning class, merchants and priests. The majority of painters and sculptors working in the private factories and in the small workshops of the Gzhel region around Moscow were the children of peasants and serfs. It was natural that their tastes and views should be reflected in the objects they created. Thus, figurines of the time tell us a good deal about the morals, customs and problems of nineteenth-century Russia.

The end of the nineteenth century saw a decline in Russia's porcelain industry, which by then was chiefly in the hands of one man, Mikhail Kuznetsov. The production of porcelain sculpture decreased sharply. Only the Imperial Porcelain Factory continued to produce figurines, many of them in the fashionable Art Nouveau style. Early twentieth-century figures, such as the 'Lady with a mask' and 'Lovers', by Konstantin Somov, and the statue of Anna Pavlova, by Seraphim Soudbinin, continued to be produced throughout the period of the Revolution.

After the October Revolution, the State Porcelain Factory began producing sculptures reflecting the new reality. First, in 1918, was a bust of Karl Marx, produced in two sizes, then, later that year, a statuette known as 'The Red Guard'. Both were designed by Vasilii Kuznetsov. The Red Guard, defender of the people's state, is the first Soviet sculpture in porcelain representing the man of the new epoch. However, it was Natalya Danko who became the acknowledged chronicler of the characters of the new Soviet era. She had been trained in the studios and workshops of four fine sculptors including Leonid Sherwood, who had studied under Rodin. Between 1909 and 1914 she studied and worked in the monumental sculpture workshop of Vasilii Kuznetsov and took part in the execution of reliefs and figures for the Russian pavilions at the World Exhibition in Rome and the International Exhibition in Turin. Kuznetsov took Danko with him when he went to Rome and Turin to oversee the final stages of both jobs and while in Italy, she was able to visit the monuments and statues of Rome, Florence, Venice and Milan. In 1914, when Kuznetsov was appointed head of the sculpture workshop at the Imperial Porcelain Factory, Danko accompanied him as his assistant. Then, in 1919, when Kuznetsov decided to leave Petrograd, she became head of the sculpture workshop, where she remained until the factory was evacuated during the Second World War.

Basing her work on the old folk traditions of Russian genre figurines, Danko set about creating statuettes with contemporary relevance. Her subjects were the people in the street and in everyday life. Men, women and children, soldiers and sailors of the Revolution, bureaucrats, gipsy fortune tellers and, later, cooperative farmers – a chronicle in porcelain of the first ten years of the Soviet state's citizens. Danko worked for 313 months at the porcelain factory, creating in that time 311 works.[19] A dozen of the best known and most popular are 'The Partisan', 'The Red Sailor', 'Sailor with Banner', 'Woman sewing a Banner', 'The Militia Woman', 'The Fortune Teller', 'Factory Woman making a Speech', 'Newspaper Boy', 'Anna Akhmatova', the 'Fifth Anniversary of the Red Army' group, 'Flower Girl' and 'Street Hooligan with Balalaika'. She also created an extraordinary chess set, known as 'The Reds and the Whites' (fig. 96). This was designed and produced in 1922–23 for exhibitions abroad, in order to earn some hard currency for the struggling new state. The Red King is represented by a worker holding a sledgehammer; the Red Queen is a peasant woman holding a sheaf of wheat. The White King is a skeleton wearing a black cloak, and the Queen a woman with a horn of plenty out of which gold pieces are spilling. The red pawns are represented by the heads of peasants, each holding a sheaf of wheat and a sickle. The white pawns are busts of slaves wrapped round with black chains. The pieces were intended to be laid out on a red and white board. This remarkable chess set was shown and sold at exhibitions in Berlin (1922) and Paris (1925), and orders for it came in from as far away as Australia. So compelling are the pieces that even individual figures, coming from broken-up sets, find ready buyers at auction.

Although the Red Army was, in theory, classless, and the officers did not wear epaulettes or other ostentatious signs of rank, it was found that soldiers still liked to receive individual awards for deeds of bravery. In 1919 an army purchasing commission from Kiev[20] bought a large collection of items from the State Porcelain Factory, including some copies of Danko's figurine 'The Partisan', to be handed out instead of medals. In his book on Danko,[21] the Soviet art historian Yuri Ovsyannikov describes how, just before the Second World War, he visited a collective farm near Kiev and was invited into the house of a farmer. Standing on the shelf in the ikon corner, known as the *krasniy ugel* (literally, the red, or beautiful, corner) was 'The Partisan'. The son of the house told him that this figurine, awarded for bravery in the war against the Whites, was his father's most cherished possession.

Suprematist Porcelain In striking contrast to the representational, often didactic, character of agitprop porcelain, the aim of the Suprematists was to build ideal, abstract forms based on the principles of economic geometry. Yet these works are usually grouped with agitprop porcelain, since the two styles are contemporaneous and because some Suprematists worked at the Lomonosov Factory. Kazimir Malevich, the leading Suprematist, designed a teapot that looks like a locomotive and some half-cups that are, literally, cups cut in half. Nikolai Suetin designed another curious teapot and a series of inkstands which look like a horizontal *arkhitekton* or space composition. The ideas were original and thought-provoking but not really very practical for the masses, and only a few such experimental pieces were produced.

Suprematists considered the colour white – and therefore white porcelain – an ideal base because it expressed weightlessness. To Malevich it also symbolized infinity. On to this white background were painted designs made up of red, yellow, black and blue triangles, rectangles, squares and circles which seem to interact and to float, defying the laws of gravity and generating remarkable energy. Malevich, Suetin and Ilia Chashnik all made designs for the decoration of plates in 1922 and 1923, and the latter two painted plates, cups and saucers themselves. Most early Suprematist work on porcelain signed by Chashnik and Suetin, or based on their designs, was made in 1923. There were several reasons for this. The 1922 exhibition in Berlin (the RSFSR's first exhibition abroad) showed that there was a tremendous interest in Russian avant-garde designs and painting. Other exhibitions in Moscow, Tallinn (Estonia), Lyons and Stockholm were planned for 1923, and the State Porcelain Factory was asked to supply items for them. Indeed, most of the Suprematist items seem to have been produced specifically for export. Chashnik and Suetin would create the prototype and factory artists would make a few dozen copies. The prototypes remained in Russia and the copies were sent abroad to earn hard currency. Most of the genuine Suprematist items seen today in foreign museums are marked 'based on a design by . . .' and dated 1923.

The Suprematists were invited to work at the factory in 1922 soon after they arrived in Petrograd from their previous base in Vitebsk. Shortly afterwards Chekhonin was asked to take over the artistic direction of the Volkhov factory, part of the Novgubfarfor group, near Novgorod, and was absent from Petrograd for most of 1923 and 1924. Several other artists went with him and this left a gap at the State Porcelain Factory which had to be filled.

Suprematism and its basic motifs – circle, square, rectangle and triangle – were taken up by many artists working with ceramics, with plates, cups and saucers in the style being produced in the late 1920s and early '30s at the Lomonosov Porcelain Factory and the Dulevo Works (formerly the Kuznetsov Works) near Moscow. Indeed, when Suetin became art director of the Lomonosov Factory in 1932, Suprematism gained a new lease of life; between 1932 and 1934 its artists were decorating plates with Suprematist designs when most painters were turning to socialist realism. The Hungarian industrial designer Eva Zeisel worked at the Lomonosov Factory in 1932, producing new forms for teapots, teacups and saucers, some of which are still in use today. Suetin was the artistic director then and she admired his sense of composition and his unerring eye. She vividly recalls working with him and once watched him spend nearly a whole day placing a small red spot on one of her vessels: 'He kept changing the size and the position of the little spot until he was satisfied, and when I looked at it, it seemed to sing.'[22]

Work on mass-produced crockery was concentrated in the Moscow area at the Dulevo and Dimitrov factories. It took a long time for the Lomonosov Factory to go into mass production because their output was commandeered by the People's Commission for Foreign Affairs [and Trade] (Narkomindel). Also, artistic porcelain and crockery represented only a small part, less than ten per cent, of the factory's output. Its chief function was to produce glass eyes, scientific instruments and fittings for electrical installations. (One of the loveliest items designed by Chekhonin is an electric isolator. It looks like a six-inch-high porcelain mushroom with the initial 'N' on it, made of exquisitely painted flowers. It would not look out of place in a display cabinet with trinkets by Fabergé.)

Design Training Experimental work and training in ceramic design and decoration was carried out at the Higher State Art-Technical Studios (VKhUTEMAS). This was the result of an attempt to set up a design school in post-revolutionary Russia and developed out of the State Free Art Studios (Svomas), founded in 1918, which it supplanted in 1920. In 1926 VKhUTEMAS became VKhUTEIN (Higher State Art-Technical Institute). VKhUTEMAS/VKhUTEIN studios existed in both Petrograd and Moscow. Experimental work also went on at the Central Artistic Ceramic Laboratory (1922–3), the Artistic Bureau of the State Experimental Institute of Silicates (GEIS, 1924–8) and the Commission for the Study of Ceramics at the State Academy of Arts (GAKhN, 1926–9).[23]

A handsome example of the pieces produced at VKhUTEMAS is a cup and saucer of Dulevo ceramic (fig. 46) decorated with a design commemorating the Third Communist International Congress by Alexander Vesnin, who was a professor in the painting department of VKhUTEMAS from 1921 to 1924. The sharp linear elements and gold, silver and black colour scheme are characteristic of Vesnin.[24] The only book in English on his work does not mention designs for porcelain, but describes in detail how 'in the spring of 1921, Vesnin and Popova worked on a project [not realized] for the sets of the mass festival, "Struggle and Victory of the Soviets" in honour of the Third Komintern Congress [the third Communist International Congress]'.[25]

Markets for Propaganda Porcelain In 1921 the New Economic Policy (NEP) was launched. Diplomatic relations began to be normalized and foreign trade was encouraged. The Lomonosov Porcelain Factory was placed under the aegis of the Academic Centre of Scientific and Artistic Institutions of the RSFSR. At the same time Narkomindel reserved for itself the factory's entire output of artistic wares for the next five years. Services were ordered for the new Soviet embassies and hundreds of pieces were sent to applied arts and industrial fairs abroad to advertise the new regime and bring back some much-needed hard currency.

Soviet propaganda porcelain was first seen abroad at the *Erste Russische Kunst Ausstellung* (First Russian Exhibition) at the Van Diemen Gallery in Berlin in the autumn of 1922. The ceramics section included 125 plates, cups, saucers and teapots. This exhibition went on to Amsterdam in late 1922. Other exhibitions took place in Tallinn, Estonia (1922); Lyons and Stockholm (1923); Paris (the *Exposition Internationale des Arts Décoratifs et Industriels Modernes*, 1925); Lyons again (1926); Monza, Italy (1927); and finally Paris again in 1928. The pieces that had not sold in Paris in 1925 were sent to London where they were sold in a shop in Hampstead called 'Fortunate Finds'.

Detail of Altman's watercolour showing the decoration for the arch of the General Staff Building. The emblem on the banner was commemorated on the plate shown on p. 41.

Decorated agit train. The bayonetting soldier is a familiar motif which also appears on the Adamovich plate on p. 35.

Design for a cup and saucer by Liubov Popova.

Bilibin's illustration, Flying Horse, from *Jar Ptitza*.

The pre-revolutionary badge of the Agricultural Institute. The emblems of an agricultural society, including the sickle, had a definite place in Russian decorative art before the Revolution.

Propaganda porcelain was also sold at special state stores in Petrograd and Moscow. At first, the State Porcelain Factory had no shop; for, from the reign of Alexander III onwards, the output of the Imperial Factory had belonged exclusively to the Imperial household. Nothing from the Imperial Factory was ever sold, except perhaps for the occasional presentation piece sold through an antique shop by a courtier in debt. After the production side of the factory had been reorganized it was necessary to find an outlet for the products so that they could fulfil their propaganda role and earn money towards the running costs of the factory. It was decided to turn the former Korniloff porcelain shop on Nevsky Prospekt in Petrograd into a showcase for the factory. (The shop is still selling Lomonosov Porcelain Factory wares today, at 63, Nevsky Prospekt.) Despite their relatively high prices all the items sold rapidly, fully covering production costs. In fact, the fast turnover caused IZO, Narkompros, to worry that propaganda porcelain was being bought by collectors and foreigners rather than by the workers and peasants for whom it was intended.

Due to its scarcity and high cost, propaganda porcelain seldom entered the homes of the masses; nor did it help to reduce illiteracy or spread world revolution. Nevertheless, it always commanded attention. Wherever it has been displayed in special shops in Leningrad and Moscow, or at Soviet exhibitions and trade fairs abroad, agitprop porcelain's vibrant colours and unusual designs – some bold, some subtle – give it an original, vital quality. It has repelled some and attracted others but never left anyone indifferent. Whether featuring Marxist slogans or celebrating May Day with flowers and ribbons, these plates make the viewer notice and remember them, thus fulfilling the intentions of their creators.

Fakes Until the 1970s there were virtually no fakes in porcelain of the Soviet period. Several events then created the demand for fakes within the Soviet Union and abroad.

First, in the late 1970s the State Museum of Ceramics at Kuskovo announced its intention to fill the gaps in certain areas of its extensive collection of ceramics. It already had a good collection of agitprop porcelain but wanted to increase it, and even commissioned authorized copies of certain plates and dishes. The purchasing budget was large and this was known in art circles. Second, in 1984 and 1985, the exhibition 'Art into Production', – of Soviet textiles and ceramics 1917–1935 – was shown first at the Museum of Modern Art, Oxford, and then at the Crafts Council in London, to great public and critical acclaim. Third, since 1984, Christie's and Sotheby's regularly include Soviet revolutionary porcelain in their twice-yearly auctions of icons, Russian pictures and works of art, in which, since 1987, individual agitprop items regularly fetch higher prices than the most expensive Sèvres plates. For all these reasons there have been busy brushes in Moscow, Leningrad and abroad. There are now fakes in the Kuskovo collection and in museums and private collections abroad.

Porcelain emigrates quite easily. West Berlin dealers have runners in the Soviet Union. The goods are taken by courier to East Berlin. The courier then takes the U-Bahn (underground) from East to West Berlin, which is unproblematic so long as one is not travelling on an East German passport. The courier delivers the goods, collects his reward and returns East. If the plates look too new they are scratched up a bit by porcelain 'restorers' in Berlin, and then offered to dealers and museums in Europe, England and the United States. The initial approach is usually a letter with photographs or photocopies of the plates, front and reverse. On photographs and photocopies the plates look all right. It is when one holds the actual plate that the trained eye notices the mistakes of the over-zealous contemporary copyist as opposed to the original artist's work or the 1920s factory artist's copy.

Notes

1
In the Soviet Union, the word 'propaganda' has positive overtones, analogous to 'advertising'.

2
The treaty was annulled by the collapse of Germany eight months later, in November 1918.

3
Translation of Lenin's writings from *The Bolshevik Poster*, Stephen White, Yale University Press, 1988, p. 19.

4
The Mind and Face of Bolshevism, Rene Fülöp-Miller, first published in 1926, Harper and Row, 1965. p. 91.

5
Porcelain in the Early Years After the October Revolution, pamphlet printed for the Order of Lenin State History Museum, Moscow, undated, p. 23.

6
The Fine Art Department of Narkompros (Otdel izobrazitelnykh iskusstv) known by its abbreviation, IZO, was set up at the beginning of 1918 in Petrograd and Moscow. David Shterenberg was president of IZO overall, with Tatlin as deputy head of IZO in Moscow. IZO's activities incorporated all aspects of the visual arts from exhibitions to art education, including the establishment of the Petrograd and Moscow Free State Art Studios (SVOMAS). IZO was run by an Arts Board which, in Petrograd, initially consisted of Shterenberg (president), Punin (deputy head, Petrograd), Vaulin, Karev, Matveev, Altman, Chekhonin and Yatmonov. The Petrograd IZO was an artistically eclectic and rather moderate body.

7
Sovietskii Farfor 1920–1930, Lydia Andreeva, Sovietskii Khudoznik, 1975, p. 61.

8
S. Chekhonin, A. Ephros and N. Punin, Moscow State Press, 1923, p. 7.

9
La Porcelaine de la Manufacture d'Etat, Eric Gollerbach, Mospetschat, 1922, p. 13.

10
On Sunday, 9 January 1905, Father Gapon, head of a workers' society, led 200,000 St. Petersburg workers and their families to the Winter Palace. They carried crosses, ikons, religious banners and portraits of the Czar. They sang 'God Save the Czar' as they walked. They hoped to present a petition to Nicholas II, listing their hardships and requesting reforms. Instead, they found their way blocked by lines of infantry. Anxious to see the Czar, they continued to move forward. The soldiers opened fire. Hundreds were killed and thousands wounded. 'Bloody Sunday', as it came to be called, touched off the first Russian Revolution. Throughout the year there was a steady rise in demonstrations, strikes and acts of terrorism. In October a general strike was called and the Czar was forced to issue a Manifesto recognizing basic civil liberties and establishing an elected assembly or 'Duma'.

11
The name both of a magazine and a group of artists, critics and aesthetes who encouraged the development of the decorative arts, particularly in St. Petersburg, in the late 1890s and the 1900s.

12
Sovietskii Farfor 1920–1930, op. cit., pp. 99–100.

13
New Larousse Encyclopedia of Mythology, Prometheus Press, 1959.

14
Named after Mosei Uritsky (1873–1918), born into a Jewish merchant family in the Ukraine, who became a professional revolutionary and, having brought about the executions of many counter-revolutionaries, was assassinated in Petrograd.

15
Zrelische, no. 26, Moscow 1923, pp. 8–9.

16
The Mind and Face of Bolshevism, op. cit., p. 275.

17
Sovietskii Khudozhestvennye Farfor 1918–1923 Isdatelistvo Akademia Khudozhestv SSSR, Moscow, 1962, p. 97.

18
Art into Production, ed. David Elliott, Museum of Modern Art, Oxford 1984, p. 11.

19
'Iesli bi Natalya Danko Byela Dnevnik', Yuri Ovsyannikov, *Panorama Iskusstv*, no. 6, Moscow 1983, p. 21.

20
Zhisn Iskusstva, Petrograd, 1 April 1919.

21
Skultor v Krasnom Khalate, Yuri Ovsyannikov, Sovietskii Khudozhnik, 1965.

22
Conversation with the author, London 1989.

23
Art into Production, op. cit., p. 13.

24
The author was told by the curator of the Lomonosov Porcelain Factory Museum in 1988 that several designs for porcelain by A. Vesnin were for sale at a Commission Store in Moscow about eight years ago.

25
Alexandr Vesnin and Russian Constructivism, Selim Khan-Magomedov, Lund Humphries, London 1986, p. 72.

ILLUSTRATIONS

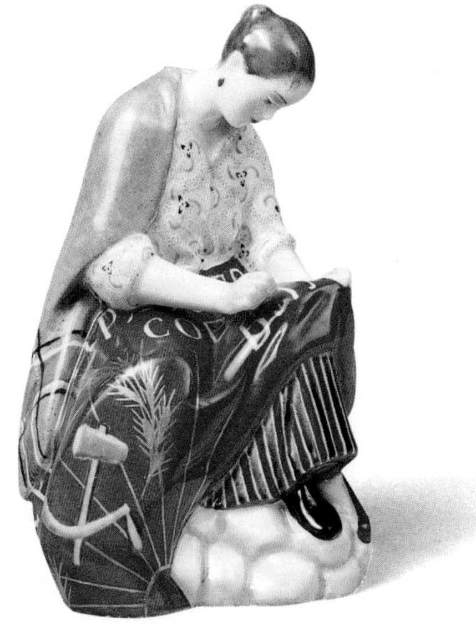

Agit Pieces

During the first years of Communism,
porcelain was used as a means of disseminating
propaganda and plates were painted with slogans.

1

1
Plate based on a design by **Mikhail M. Adamovich**
Plate decorated with the silhouette of a factory worker in iron-red, a factory and the word 'Kapital' in Cyrillic letters.
Marks:
IPF monogram for Nicholas II, 1909 in green underglaze; SPF mark of hammer, sickle and cog plus '1921' in blue overglaze. Monogram of factory artist Varvara F. Rukavishnikova in blue overglaze. Dm. 10 in. (25.5 cm.)

2
Mikhail M. Adamovich

Plate with a portrait of Lenin and the slogan 'He Who Does Not Work Does Not Eat'. The plate is also decorated with ration cards, half an imperial eagle, a red star, the word 'Lenin' and the monogram RSFSR (Russian Soviet Federated Socialist Republic). The portrait is based on a famous sketch by Natan I. Altman which was one of the few portraits of Lenin taken from life. In the earlier versions of the plate, like the one shown below, the red star is on top of the eagle, obliterating it. The plate typifies the life of the time: colourful, uncertain and full of contrasts.

Marks:
IPF monogram for Nicholas II, 1898 in green underglaze; SPF mark of hammer, sickle and cog plus '1923' in blue overglaze. Also, pattern number: 506/12 in blue overglaze. No signature. The prototype of this plate was created in 1921.
Dm. $9\frac{3}{4}$ in. (25 cm.)

3

Dish based on a design by **Mikhail M. Adamovich**
Dish, 'Fifth Anniversary of the Red Army', prototype created in 1923. The cavetto is painted with a Red Army soldier standing on the time-honoured emblems of czarist Russia, the Imperial crown and a banner with the Romanov eagle, inherited from Byzantium. Golden oak leaves circle the cavetto. The Roman numeral 'V' appears twice, with the dates, 1918–1923, and exquisitely painted flowers form the interlaced monogram, 'RSFSR'.
Marks:
IPF monogram for Nicholas II, 1904 in green underglaze; SPF mark of hammer, sickle and cog, plus '1925' in blue overglaze.
Dm. 12 in. (30 cm.)

4

Mikhail M. Adamovich
Plate, 'Long Live the Red Army 1918–1923'.
The cavetto of the plate is decorated with a Red Army soldier trampling upon and bayonetting the British and Japanese flags (representing the British and Japanese interventionist forces) as well as Imperial yellow banners bearing the names of the White generals Yudenich, Wrangel, Deniken and Dietrikhs and that of Admiral Kolchak. The letters RSFSR appear on a map of Russia between the soldier's feet. A golden Roman V indicates that it is the fifth anniversary of the Red Army. The cobalt-blue margin of the plate is decorated with golden stars and oxidized silver Cyrillic letters spell out 'Long Live the Red Army'.
Marks:
IPF monogram for Nicholas II, 1911 in green underglaze; special mark for fifth anniversary of Red Army consisting of a hammer, sickle and cog, and a red star plus 1923, painted by Adamovich, and his signature, 'M. Adamovich" in Cyrillic, all in overglaze.
Also, 'No.1171'. Dm. 9½ in. (24 cm.)

5
Mikhail M. Adamovich
Plate celebrating the Fifth Anniversary of the Red Army and honouring its creator, Trotsky. In the cobalt-blue border decorated with oak leaves (for valour), Cyrillic letters proclaim 'Hail to the Red Army'. Within the cavetto there is a portrait of Trotsky, a red star with crossed hammer and sickle, a facsimile of Trotsky's signature, and a worker and Red Army soldier holding a sign which reads '1917 Red Army 1922'. They also hold a golden wheel with the numeral '5' in the centre and '23 October, Moscow 1917'. Underneath, in iron-red script are the words 'Defence of the Workers'.
Marks:
IPF monogram for Nicholas II, 1896 in green underglaze; SPF mark of hammer, sickle and cog, plus '1924' and '408/6' in blue overglaze. Dm. 9½ in. (24 cm.)

6
Mikhail M. Adamovich
Four coffee cups and matching saucers known as 'Lenin with Red Star'. They are decorated with a famous portrait of Lenin; marching soldiers, the date, '25 Oct. 1917', the letters 'RSFSR', a hammer and sickle and a large red star. The portrait of Lenin is based on a sketch by Natan Altman. The five-pointed red star containing a handplough and a hammer appears on many of Adamovich's plates and cups. It is the symbol of the worker-peasant Red Army in which Adamovich served.
Marks:
Cup I IPF mark for Alexander III, 744894 in green underglaze; SPF mark of hammer, sickle and cog and '1922' in blue overglaze, plus number 'N 3/24'.
Cup II IPF mark for Alexander III, 1889 (unclear) in green underglaze; rest same as above except for number which is 'N 3/22'.
Cup III IPF mark for Alexander III, 744894 in green underglaze; SPF mark of hammer, sickle and cog and '1922' in blue overglaze, plus pattern number 'N.3/21'.
Cup IV IPF mark for Alexander III, 744894 in green underglaze; SPF mark of hammer, sickle and cog and '1922', plus pattern number 'N.3/13', all in blue overglaze. Height (all four) 3 in. (7.5 cm.)
Saucer I Imperial Porcelain Factory mark for Alexander III, 1889 in green underglaze; State Porcelain Factory mark of hammer, sickle, cog and '1922' in blue overglaze, plus 'N. 3/23' in blue overglaze.
Saucer II Same as above except for the number which is 'N.3/21'.
Saucer III Same as above except for the number which is 'N.3/19'.
Saucer IV Same as above except that the State Porcelain Factory mark consists only of a hammer and sickle, '1922' and 'N.3/13', all in blue overglaze. Dm. (all four) 6¼ in. (15.7 cm.)

These are all hand-painted, not done by transfer print, so although the design is the same there are slight variations in the execution from item to item. For instance the little circle within the red star is sometimes more, sometimes less filled with a green and black circle and a dot.

Mikhail M. Adamovich
Plate known as 'The Volunteer'. One of the two soldiers is a
self-portrait of the artist. The back is inscribed in Cyrillic, in the
artist's hand, in iron-red overglaze: 'War 1920–1921, Western
Front, Red Army in the trenches of the Russian–German War
at Lida-Cholodetcheno. Painted by the participant in the Great
War and ex-Red soldier M. Adamovich.'

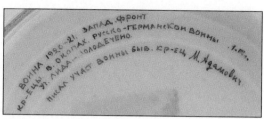

Marks:
IPF monogram for Nicholas II, 1915 in green underglaze; SPF
mark of hammer, sickle and cog plus '1921' in blue overglaze.
Dm. $8\frac{9}{16}$ in. (21.8 cm.)

8

Mikhail M. Adamovich

Plate sometimes called 'Wounded' and sometimes 'Commissary Supplies'. It shows a night scene consisting of a soldier in Red Army uniform sitting by a fire with a wounded combatant wearing a fur hat. In the background there is a square, stone tower (perhaps a granary?) against which are silhouetted a mounted sentry and other figures. (In 1921 Adamovich produced a series of drawings and watercolours based on his observations and experiences during his years in the Red Army, 1919–21. According to the Soviet authority Lydia Andreeva, he executed this series in a deep-green or brick-red tone reminiscent of the drawings of the Romantic School of the 1820s and '30s. Several of the series were used to decorate plates.)
Marks:
IPF monogram for Nicholas II, 1905 in green underglaze; SPF mark of hammer, sickle and cog plus '1921' in green overglaze. 'Po riz Khud. Adamovicha' (based on drawing by artist Adamovich) in Cyrillic, in blue overglaze, plus initials of factory artist 'Ap' in Cyrillic – that is, 'Ar' – also in blue overglaze (unidentified). Dm. 9$\frac{15}{16}$ in. (25.2 cm.)

9

Mikhail M. Adamovich

Plate known as 'Bivouac'. The cavetto is decorated with a soldier wearing the distinctive, peaked Red Army head-dress with sideflaps and a red star on it, and two other men with shaggy fur hats – perhaps Azerbaijanis. In the background is the silhouette of a man on a horse, a huge camel and a hayrick. The men are sitting around a fire. They are probably guarding the harvest. 1921 was a time of severe famine in Russia.
Marks:
IPF monogram for Nicholas II, 1904 in green underglaze; SPF mark of hammer, sickle plus '1921', scratched in but not painted; the cog is painted in blue overglaze. Also 'Po rizunku Khud. Adamovicha' (based on drawing by artist Adamovich) in blue overglaze, plus initials of factory artist 'Ap' in Cyrillic (Ar). Dm. 10 in. (25.5 cm.)

8

9

Mikhail M. Adamovich

Plate with a slogan 'Long Live the Third International!' in German, circling the shaped border. The cavetto is decorated with a flower-adorned hammer and sickle plus '25 October 1917 Year' in Cyrillic, all caught up in a whirlpool effect.

Adamovich often used this particular iron-red. The whirlpool effect may symbolize the whirlwind events of the period.
Marks:
IPF monogram for Nicholas II, 1905 in green underglaze; SPF mark of hammer, sickle and cog plus '1921' in blue overglaze. Adamovich's monogram AM in blue overglaze on reverse.
Dm. 9¾ in. (25 cm.)

11

Natan I. Altman

Plate, 'The Land Is For The Workers'. The green field is decorated with a red rhombus enclosing a red factory, sickle and stalk of wheat. The slogan circles the border in large red letters. Several identical plates, a few drawings, and descriptions by contemporary witnesses are all that remain as evidence of Altman's extraordinary transformation of Palace Square, the Winter Palace, and the General Staff Arch and Building on the first anniversary of the October Revolution. The motif in the cavetto of the plate commemorates that which decorated the immense banner that hung under the arch of the General Staff Building.

This plate was based on a design by Altman but was not painted by him; he did not paint on porcelain. According to his widow, the colours green and red were specifically chosen to represent the land and the workers. Everything has been carefully thought out – the clear, strong lettering, and the equal space and value accorded to the two colours.
Marks:
SPF mark of hammer, sickle and cog plus '1919' in grey overglaze. (The plate looks and feels like a plate manufactured by the IPF; however, it bears only the marks of the SPF.)
Dm. 9⅝ in. (24.5 cm.)

12

Sergei V. Chekhonin (Tchekhonine)

Plate with interlaced Cyrillic letters 'RSFSR' (Russian Soviet Federated Socialist Republic). Note how the Cyrillic versions of 'S' (C) have little handles on them, turning them into sickles. Prototype created in 1919.

Services made at the imperial and royal factories of Berlin, Sèvres and Vienna in the eighteenth century, were frequently adorned with monograms consisting of interlaced letters made up of small flowers. Similar monograms were painted at the Imperial Porcelain Factory during the reign of Catherine II, and Chekhonin was undoubtedly inspired by all these eighteenth-century examples.

Marks:
IPF monogram for Nicholas II, 1894 in green underglaze; SPF mark of hammer, sickle and cog plus '1921' in blue overglaze. Dm. 10½ in. (26.6 cm.)

13

Sergei V. Chekhonin (Tchekhonine)

Plate with a large star surrounded by stylized Cyrillic letters proclaiming: 'The Kingdom of the Workers and the Peasants Shall Have No End'. Within the star more letters spell the word 'Kommuna'. The prototype of this plate was created in 1919.

Marks:
IPF mark for Nicholas II, 1898 in green underglaze; SPF mark of hammer, sickle and cog plus '1920' in blue overglaze. Dm. 9½ in. (24 cm.)

14

Plate based on design by **Sergei V. Chekhonin (Tchekhonine)**

Plate, 'From the Heights of Science it is easier to see the Dawn of the new Day than from below amidst the Mists of Everyday Life', in Cyrillic letters, encircling a hammer and sickle.

Marks:
SPF mark of hammer, sickle and cog, plus '1921' in blue overglaze. Dm. 9½ in. (24 cm.)

15

Dish based on a design by **Sergei V. Chekhonin (Tchekhonine)**

Dish, 'RSFSR. The Kingdom of the Workers and the Peasants Will Have No End'. (Prototype created 1920.)

Marks:

IPF monogram for Nicholas II, 1913 in green underglaze, and special Fifth Anniversary of SPF mark, designed by Chekhonin, consisting of crossed hammer and sickle with a Roman numeral 'V' crowned by a cog. Date, '1922', plus 'N.1.10.', all in blue overglaze. Dm. 12¼ in. (31 cm.)

16

Sergei V. Chekhonin (Tchekhonine)

A huge platter known as the 'Signature Platter'. The date, 1917, appears at the top of the cavetto. The centre part is covered with elegantly designed, multi-coloured Cyrillic letters which read 'Autographs Of The Architects Of The Great Russian October Revolution'. The lower part of the cavetto is decorated with a hammer and sickle on either side of a section of the globe representing Russia. A twirling red ribbon and oak leaves circle the cavetto. (Oak and laurel leaves are traditionally for heroes. The red ribbon derives from the design of the Service for the Knights of the Order Of St. Alexander Nevsky, from the Gardner Factory, commissioned by Catherine II in 1777 and completed in 1780.) The border is decorated with leaves and seventeen facsimile signatures. Starting at the bottom and going clockwise, they are A. Enukidze, V. Yakovleva, V. Volodarsky, G. Zinoviev, L. Trotsky, M. Uritsky, K. Eremeev, A. Riazanov, N. Krestinsky, A. Lunacharsky, V. Ulyanov (Lenin), G. Chicherin, A. Kollontai, Vlad. Bonch-Bruevich, S. Gusev and S. Zorin. Between Uritsky and Eremeev, there is an indecipherable signature. Some people read it as Podbelsky. It is interesting to note that neither Stalin's nor Bukharin's signature is included. The platter illustrates several of Chekhonin's styles of calligraphy, as well as his various ways of adorning letters.

The Signature Platter was brought back to England by Captain Desmond Allhusen who was Assistant British Agent in Moscow in the early twenties. In 1923, Captain Allhusen, in company with Sir Robert Hodgson, the British Agent, visited the State Porcelain Shop in Moscow, where it was purchased. Lydia Andreeva, shown photographs of the platter, said that she had never seen one like it in the Soviet Union.

Marks:

IPF monogram for Nicholas II, 1904 in green underglaze; SPF mark of hammer and sickle (unclear) in blue overglaze. Also, 'Po Chekhoninu' (based on Chekhonin) in Cyrillic letters, in white, reversed out of the black border at the front of the platter. Height: 21¼ in. (54 cm.) Width: 15¼ in. (38.5 cm.)

17

Sergei V. Chekhonin (Tchekhonine)

Plate bearing Lenin's head surrounded by a red ribbon and oak leaves. The Cyrillic letters on the ribbon proclaim 'Proletariat of All The World Unite'. Under Lenin's portrait is his name, 'V. Ulianov', in Cyrillic.

Marks:

IPF monogram obliterated with an oval green blob; SPF mark of hammer, sickle and cog plus '1920' in blue overglaze.

Dm. 12⅛ in. (31 cm.)

18

Sergei V. Chekhonin (Tchekhonine)

Dish, 'The Decembrists', created in 1925 for the 100th anniversary of the Decembrist uprising in 1825. In the centre of the plate is a group portrait, in profile, of the five Decembrists who were executed: Pavel Pestel, Kondrati Ryleyev, Sergei Muravyov-Apostol, Mikhail Bestuzhev-Riumin and Pyotr Kakhovsky (the others were sent to Siberia). Their portrait is surrounded by a red aura and a garland of oak leaves. The Cyrillic inscription circling the plate reads, top: 'You Did Not Die In Vain'; bottom: 'What You Sowed Will Grow'.

Marks:

IPF monogram for Alexander III, 1893; SPF mark of hammer, sickle and cog, and '1926' in blue overglaze. Dm. 13 in. (33.1 cm.)

Sergei V. Chekhonin (Tchekhonine)

Early propaganda plate. The border is circled with the slogan 'The Task Of Science Is To Serve People', in Cyrillic letters, and a stylized hammer and sickle.
Marks:
Provisional Government mark obliterated with a round, green blob; SPF mark of hammer, sickle and cog plus '1918', in blue overglaze. Dm. 9½ in. (24 cm.) (The Provisional Government mark, consisting of a tiny double-headed eagle without a crown within a hyphenated circle, was used for only about six months in 1917 and early 1918. It was designed by Ivan Bilibin.)

Sergei V. Chekhonin (Tchekhonine)

Early propaganda plate. The border is circled with the slogan, 'The Mind Cannot Tolerate Slavery', in Cyrillic letters.
Marks:
Provisional Government mark obliterated by a round, green blob; SPF mark of hammer, sickle and cog plus '1918' in greyish-blue overglaze. Dm. 9⅝ in. (24.5 cm.) (See note for plate 19, describing the Provisional Government mark.)

19

20

Sergei V. Chekhonin (Tchekhonine)
Large dish known as 'Famine'. It portrays a grieving mother/
madonna in a black and gold veil. She has a ravaged, pale-green
face and is holding two pale-green starving children. This dish
came out of the Soviet Union with Chekhonin when he
emigrated to France in 1928. It is unique. Chekhonin considered
it one of his masterpieces.
Marks:
IPF monogram for Nicholas II, 1913 in green underglaze; SPF
mark of hammer, sickle and cog in black overglaze. Signed by
the artist: 'Sergei Chekhonin 1921' in Cyrillic, on both the front
and the reverse, in black overglaze. Dm. 12 in. (31 cm.)
22
Sergei V. Chekhonin (Tchekhonine)
Large dish known as 'Sorrow'. The border is cobalt blue. The
cavetto contains a lovely maiden, perhaps Ceres, perhaps
Russia, holding a cornucopia in her right arm from which black
leaves flutter. The maiden is grieving for the catastrophic
harvest, hence the black leaves instead of grain. This is the
prototype, painted by the master's hand, of a dish which was
repeated by factory artists and which one sees in several
museums in the Soviet Union. The prototype came out of the
Soviet Union with Chekhonin when he emigrated.
Marks:
IPF monogram for Alexander III, 1893 in green underglaze; SPF
mark of hammer, sickle and cog, beautifully painted in blue
overglaze by Chekhonin, plus date '1921' and the initials 'S.Ch.'
in Cyrillic, in black overglaze. The front of the plate is signed
'Sergei Chekhonin 1921'. Dm. 13¼ in. (33.5 cm.)

21

23
Liubov N. Gaush

A large, oval platter with an undulating green swag in its border and colourful flowers, plus the Cyrillic letters 'RSFSR' (Russian Soviet Federated Socialist Republic) in the cavetto. The letters are decorated with little flowers engraved in the gold.

Marks:
IPF monogram for Nicholas II, 1908 in green underglaze; SPF mark of hammer, sickle and cog in blue overglaze. Cyrillic initials for L.G., plus date, '1921', in blue overglaze.
Length: 17½ in. (44.2 cm.) Width: 12¼ in. (31.5 cm.)

24
Natalya A. Girshfeld

Dish inscribed 'Petrograd 1921'. This is one of the twenty-three items, specially created by artists at the SPF, in aid of the Volga region famine victims in 1921. The black letters and black ears of wheat indicate Petrograd's mourning, both for the dead and for the desolate, parched Volga region.

Marks:
IPF monogram for Nicholas II, 1896 in green underglaze; the special famine mark designed by Chekhonin, painted in gold (see chart of marks at back) and Cyrillic initials 'N.G.' Dm. 14 in. (35.5 cm.)

23

24

25

Alisa R. Golenkina

Plate with torch-bearing man on a winged horse flying over collapsing classical monuments in flames. The border is circled by a slogan in German, 'We Shall Set The World Ablaze With The Fire Of The Third International'. (A similar plate with the slogan in Russian can be seen at the Lenin State History Museum on Red Square.)

Marks:

IPF monogram for Nicholas II, 1898 in green underglaze; SPF mark of hammer, sickle and cog plus '1922', in grey overglaze. Pattern number '242/6' in grey overglaze. Dm. 9⅜ in. (23.8 cm.)

25

26

Zinaida V. Kobyletskaya

Plate known as 'History of the October Revolution, 1917'. The cavetto is decorated with an open book thus inscribed, plus 'Petersburg 1921' and a copy of the newspaper *Petrogradskaya Pravda*. A golden sickle encircles half the cavetto and the books are decorated with and surrounded by the exquisite flowers, leaves and grasses for which Kobyletskaya is known.
Marks:
IPF monogram for Nicholas II in green underglaze; SPF mark of hammer, sickle and cog plus '1921'. Dm. 8¾ in. (22.3 cm.)

27

Zinaida V. Kobyletskaya

A large plate decorated with leaves, ferns, grasses, a star and the slogan 'In Unity Is Our Strength', in Cyrillic letters. Front of plate signed 'Z. Kobyletskaya' in Cyrillic, amongst some leaves on the border.
Marks:
IPF monogram for Nicholas II, 1901 in green underglaze; SPF mark of hammer, sickle and cog plus '1921' in green overglaze, and the artist's mark, a cross within a circle.
Dm. 11¾ in. (30 cm.)

26

27

28
Dish based on design by **Zinaida V. Kobyletskaya**
Dish known as 'Newspapers', Petrograd 1921. It shows a
colourful assemblage of fourteen newspapers and periodicals,
and an educational poster. The titles are painted with precision
and are easy to read: the *Petrosoviet News, The Red Commander,
Trud, The Red Way, Village Pravda, Izvestia, The Art of the
Commune, The Life of Art, The Red Baltic Navy,* an educational
poster setting out the new spelling system, the *Petrograd Pravda,*
the *Red Gazette, The Fly-wheel,* and *The Baltic Sea Transport,*
together with one unidentified newspaper. On the front of *The
Red Commander,* a Red Army soldier holds a banner reading,
'Proletariat of the World Unite'.

   During the period of famine, newspapers were widely held
to represent the nourishment of the period, and so would be
considered as appropriate decoration for a dish. They are
surrounded by a border of leaves interspersed with Cyrillic
letters which spell 'Petrograd 1921'.
Marks:
IPF monogram for Nicholas II, 1907 in green underglaze; SPF
mark of hammer, sickle and cog, plus 1921, in black overglaze.
The initials E. Ya. (Ekaterina Yakimovskaya) and 'Po riz
Kobyletskaya' (based on design by Kobyletskaya), all in Cyrillic.
Dm. 14$\frac{1}{2}$ in.(36.8 cm.)

29
Zinaida V. Kobyletskaya
Plate with a red star made up of iron-red leaf-shaped paint
daubs. The slogan 'Long Live Soviet Power' circles the border.
Marks:
IPF monogram for Nicholas II, 1910 in green underglaze; SPF
mark of hammer, sickle and cog plus '1921' in blue overglaze.
No signature. Dm. 9$\frac{1}{4}$ in. (23.5 cm.)

Plate based on design by **Maria V. Lebedeva**

Large plate painted with a red star in the centre of which is the head of a tchekist (member of the secret police). The border is decorated with palaces interspersed with factories (the old and the new) and the quotation, 'I see plots everywhere of the rich seeking their own profit in the name, and under the pretext of Good.' The red star represents the Soviet State and its points are lodged in the factories from which it draws its strength – the workers.

Marks:

IPF monogram for Nicholas II, 1913 in green underglaze; SPF mark of hammer and sickle plus '1922' in blue overglaze. Dm. 12⅜ in. (31.5 cm.)

Maria V. Lebedeva

Plate with slogan 'Life Without Work is Thievery', circling the border in Cyrillic letters. The cavetto is decorated with a gypsy woman reading the hand of an elegant young lady. The subject may be ironic for gypsies are not famous for their hard work. Front of the plate signed 'Maria Lebedeva', in Cyrillic, in green overglaze.

Marks:

IPF monogram obliterated with diamond-shaped green patch; SPF mark of hammer, sickle and cog plus '1921' in green overglaze. Also, Maria Lebedeva's monogram, a capital M with a swan nesting in it (*lebedev* is the Russian word for swan), in green overglaze. Dm. 9.5 in. (24 cm.)

30

31

32

Maria V. Lebedeva
Large platter known as 'The Telephonist'.
Marks:
SPF mark of hammer, sickle and cog, 1920 and Lebedeva's
monogram, a swan nesting on the letter M, in blue overglaze.
LPF inventory letters and the number, 1811.

32

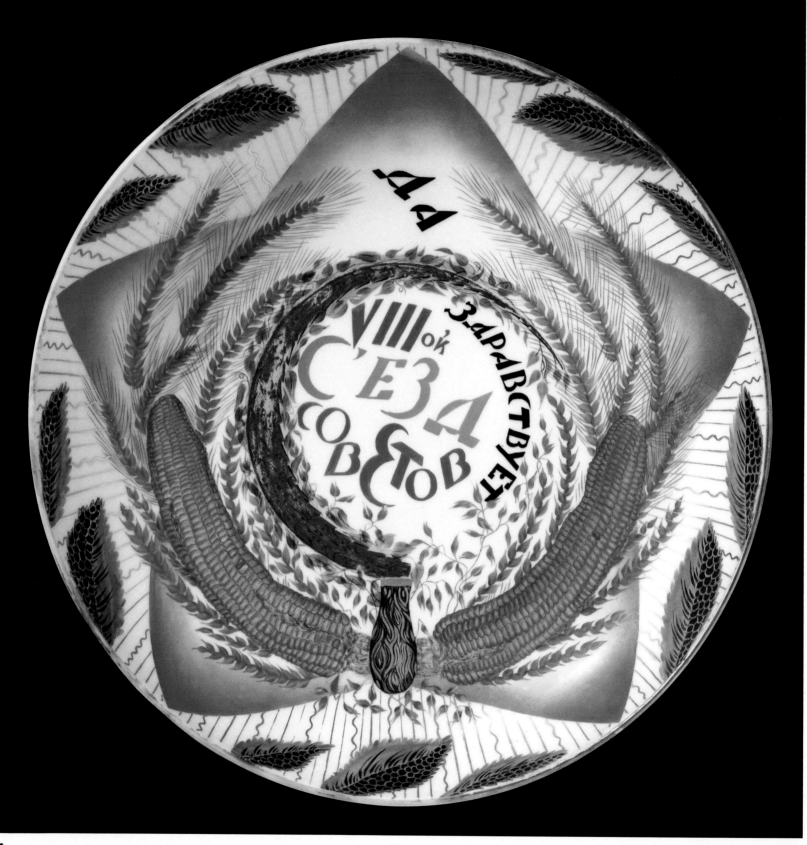

33

Bazilka S. Radonich

Platter, 'The Transparent Star'. One of many works designed by different artists to celebrate the Eighth Congress of the Soviets. The Cyrillic lettering proclaims: 'Hail to the Eighth Congress of the Soviets'.

Marks:

IPF monogram for Alexander III 1892, in green underglaze; SPF factory mark of hammer, sickle and cog plus '1920' and the Cyrillic initial B (Bazilka), all in blue overglaze.

Dm. 14⅛ in. (36 cm.)

34

Bazilka S. Radonich

Tray, known as 'The New Government'.

Circling the tray in gold Cyrillic letters on a blue background are the abbreviated words, 'Ross. Soc. Fed. Sov. Resp.' (Russian Socialist Federated Soviet Republic). Issuing from a rose-red and gold cornucopia are colourful flowers containing the acronyms of ten government departments and agencies: IZO, TCHEKA, ISPOLKOM, DOMKOMBED, KOMPROS, KOMPROD, CIK, RABISSO, SOVNARKOM, and VSEVOBOUCH.

Marks:

1921 and 'B' (for Bazilka).

Dm. 13⅞ in. (35.2 cm.)

35

Yelizaveta B. Rozendorf

Plate with slogan 'Long Live The Eighth Congress of the Soviets, 1920' circling the border in Cyrillic letters. The cavetto is encircled by the blade of a sickle and its centre is decorated with hammer, pliers and a factory. Rozendorf was prolific in the production of agitprop designs. Note the skilful decorative use of the sickle as both tool and frame.

Marks:

IPF monogram obliterated by an oval green blob; SPF mark of hammer, sickle and cog plus '1920' in blue overglaze.

Dm. 9½ in. (24 cm.)

34

35

36

Alexandra V. Shchekotikhina-Pototskaya

Plate known as 'The Commissar'. The Cyrillic letters circling the border spell out: 'Uritsky Square – Petrograd 1921'. One sees the General Staff Building and the Alexander Column. (Heads of government departments in the Soviet Union were known as commissars rather than ministers until 1946.) This is a well-known plate which was repeated many times by Shchekotikhina-Pototskaya and by factory artists. Uritsky Square was called Palace Square before the Revolution, and is again known by this name today.

Marks:

IPF monogram for Nicholas II, 1912 in green underglaze, with a line drawn through it in blue overglaze; SPF mark of hammer and sickle in blue overglaze. Initials 'A.Shch.' in Cyrillic, in blue overglaze. Dm. 9$\frac{3}{8}$ in. (23.7 cm.)

37

Alexandra V. Shchekotikhina-Pototskaya

Plate, 'The Sailor Takes a Walk', showing a sailor with his girlfriend. The sailor's hat is inscribed 'Baltflot', for Baltic Fleet, in Cyrillic. The border is inscribed in gold Cyrillic letters, 'celebrating 1 May in Petrograd [in the] year 1921'.

Marks:

IPF monogram for Alexander III in green underglaze; SPF mark of hammer, sickle and cog plus '1921' in blue overglaze and inscribed, in Cyrillic, 'po riz Shchekotikinoi' (based on design by Shchekotikhina), plus initials 'M.K.' (factory artist Maria P. Kirilova). Dm. 13$\frac{5}{8}$ in. (34.5 cm.)

38

Plate based on design by **Alexandra V. Shchekotikhina-Pototskaya**

Plate 'History (of the) Revolution 1917'. This plate has four books and a sledgehammer in its cavetto and is entirely covered with colourful dancing letters. They proclaim, in Russian, 'To All Who are Brave and Young at Heart [put] into their Hands a Book, a Sickle and a Hammer', plus the date, 1921. The slogan comes from an old Russian saying which people used to utter when in the presence of a clever child, 'into his hands a book'. The Soviets have grafted a sickle and a hammer onto the older Russian saying. Furthermore, they have managed to make a rhyme out of it with *molod* (young) and *molot* (hammer).

Marks:

IPF monogram for Nicholas II, 1898 in green underglaze. SPF mark of hammer, sickle and cog, plus '1921' in blue overglaze. Dm. 9$\frac{1}{2}$ in. (24 cm.)

36

37

39

Platter based on drawing by Alexandra V. Shchekotikhina-Pototskaya

Oval platter with inscription 'Present Revolutionary Thought is Socialism', circling the edge in multi-coloured and gold Cyrillic letters. Scattered about the centre more Cyrillic letters state 'Socialism, the Religion of Man, is on Earth, not in Heaven', a quotation from Lunacharsky. In the large letters spelling 'Socialism' there are a bricklayer, a man with a spade and a girl carrying a jar of water on her head. Within the two medallions we have, at the top, believers in front of idols, used here as symbols of religion, and below people at a puppet show. The platter is intended as a celebration of life and the beauty of nature, represented by flowers and foliage.

Marks:

IPF monogram for Alexander III, 1887 in green underglaze; SPF mark of hammer, sickle and cog, plus '1923' and 'N 536/3' in blue overglaze. Also, in Cyrillic, 'based on drawing of Shchekotikhina' and initials 'MK' (factory artist Maria Kirilova) in blue overglaze. Length 17¼ in. (44 cm.)

40

Plate based on design by **Alexandra V. Shchekotikhina-Pototskaya**

Plate with shaped border, green leaves, ears of wheat and the date, 1921.

This plate commemorates the dreadful famine of 1921 in the Volga Region. Hence the sinister black numbers and the limp, broken stems of wheat representing the scorched, barren Volga basin and its starving populace. Nature in Shchekotikhina's works is usually fruitful and forceful. On this plate it is represented as sterile and withered. It is reminiscent of Moor's powerful black and white lithographic poster 'Pomogi' (Help), showing a gigantic, emaciated peasant whose body is transfixed by a dried-out broken blade of wheat.
Marks:
IPF monogram obliterated with an oval black blob. SPF mark of hammer, sickle and cog, plus '1921' in blue overglaze.
Dm. 9¾ in. (25 cm.)

41

Plate based on design by **Alexandra V. Shchekotikhina-Pototskaya**

Plate on which the gold and multi-coloured Cyrillic letters spell out 'Fifth Anniversary of the October Revolution', with the dates, 1917–1922, and 'RSFSR' (Russian Soviet Federated Socialist Republic).
Marks:
IPF monogram for Alexander III, 1889 in green underglaze; SPF mark of hammer, sickle and cog plus '1922' in blue overglaze. Monogram for factory artist Varvara Feodorovna Rukavishnikova in blue overglaze. Dm. 12 in. (30.5 cm.)

40

41

42
Plate based on a design by **Alexandra V. Shchekotikhina-Pototskaya**
Plate, 'The Bellringer'. The Cyrillic lettering in the cavetto proclaims 'Long Live the Eighth Congress of the Soviets', and is surrounded by a decorated wooden bell frame, leaves and pealing bells. This is one of numerous works designed to celebrate the Eighth Congress.
Marks:
IPF monogram for Nicholas II in green underglaze; SPF mark of hammer, sickle and cog, plus '1921' in blue overglaze.
Dm. 11 in. (28 cm.)

43
Oganes K. Tatevosyan
Teacup and saucer commemorating the Congress of the People of the East, which took place in Baku, September 1920, under the chairmanship of Zinoviev. The saucer shows five representatives of the different peoples of the East holding hands around a red star containing a hammer and sickle. Both cup and saucer bear the VKhUTEMAS mark. (See note for cup and saucer by Vesnin for description and explanation of VKhUTEMAS.)
Marks:
Cup VKhUTEMAS mark in iron red. Height 3 in. (7.5 cm.)
Saucer VKhUTEMAS mark in iron red. Dm. 5½ in. (14.3 cm.)

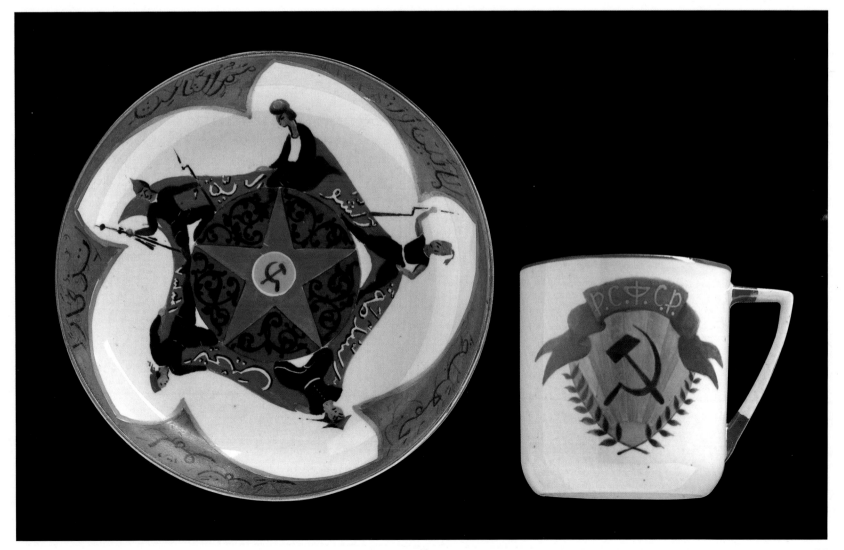

43

44
Vasilii P. Timorev

Dish with torch-bearing Red Army soldier striding over mountains and a mosque to bring enlightenment to the peoples of the East. Around the cavetto, anti-clockwise and to be read from right to left, are inscriptions in Chinese, Arabic and Turkish. The Arabic inscription is a mirror-image. Chinese: 'Wretched Workers of the World Unite'; Arabic: 'Wretches of the World Unite'; Turkish: 'The Assembly of all the Easterners of the World'.
Marks:
IPF monogram for Nicholas II, 1906 in green underglaze; SPF mark of hammer, sickle and cog, plus Timorev's trefoil mark, all in blue overglaze. Dm. $14\frac{1}{4}$ in. (36 cm.)

45
Vasilii P. Timorev

Dish with a profile of Grigori Evseevich Zinoviev in its centre surrounded by seven figures in Central Asian costumes. They, in turn, are encircled by iron-red, stylized Cyrillic lettering proclaiming: 'The People Of The East Rally Under The Leadership Of Zinoviev in Baku'. The seven figures probably represent Uzbekistan, Turkmenistan, Tadzhikistan, Kirgiziya, Kazakistan, Armenia and Azerbaijan, all Soviet Socialist Republics.

G. E. Zinoviev (1883–1936) was born in the Ukraine into a lower middle-class Jewish family. As a Russian revolutionary leader he was for many years one of Lenin's chief collaborators. Between 1919 and 1926 he was chairman of the executive committee of the Communist (Third) International, and therefore its single most powerful representative. He was executed by Stalin in the Great Purge of the 1930s. His real name was Ovshi Gershon Aronovich Radomyslsky.
Marks:
IPF monogram for Alexander III, 1893; SPF mark of hammer, sickle and cog in blue overglaze. Signature 'Timorev 22.XI.', in black overglaze, plus Timorev's trefoil mark in blue overglaze. Also Cyrillic initials 'G.O.' in blue overglaze (unidentified) plus an 'N' with two strokes through it, in blue overglaze and pattern number '405' in black overglaze. Dm. $14\frac{1}{4}$ in. (36 cm.)

Cup and saucer based on a design by **Alexander A. Vesnin**

Teacup and saucer of Dulevo ceramic decorated in gold and black with multi-coloured banners and the words 'Au III Congrés Comintern' (To the Third Comintern Congress) on the cup. The Dulevo factory is near Moscow.

Marks:

'BXYTEMAC' in iron-red overglaze with 'KERFAK' (Ceramic Manufacture) below it, and a stylized figure at a potter's wheel within the arch formed by the two acronyms. 'BXYTEMAC' is the Cyrillic spelling for VKhUTEMAS, the abbreviation and acronym for 'Vyshie gosudarstvennye kdudozhestvennotekhni-cheskie masterskie' (The Higher State Artistic and Technical Workshops).

Cup Height 2⅛ in. (5.5 cm.)
Saucer Dm. 5¾ in. (14.5 cm.)

47

Coffee can and saucer based on design of **Rudolf F. Vilde** or **Sergei V. Chekhonin**

Coffee can and saucer decorated with stylized Cyrillic letters for RSFSR. Various authorities are divided as to who designed these pieces. Lydia Andreeva does not think they are by Chekhonin.

Marks:

Cup SPF mark of hammer, sickle and cog plus '1923' and pattern number '13/54', all in blue overglaze. Height $2\frac{3}{4}$ in. (7 cm.)

Saucer Blurred SPF mark of hammer, sickle and cog plus '1919' in green underglaze. Dm. $5\frac{1}{2}$ in. (14 cm.)

48

Rudolf F. Vilde

Plate containing the emblem of the republic and a fluttering red banner with the slogan 'Victory to the Workers – 25th Oct.' Above the banner are the dates, 1917–1919. The elegant cobalt-blue border is decorated with leaves, flowers and working tools beautifully executed in scratched gold and oxidized silver. When the blade of the sickle is rubbed clean the letters RSFSR (Russian Soviet Federated Socialist Republic) appear.

Marks:

SPF mark of hammer, sickle and cog plus '1920' in blue overglaze. (The plate looks and feels like a plate manufactured by the IPF, but only bears the mark of the SPF.) No signature. Dm. $9\frac{3}{4}$ in. (25 cm.)

49

50

51

52

49

Plate, probably by **Rudolf F. Vilde**

Plate with a hammer and sickle. The word 'Russia' in Cyrillic letters at the top, the dates '1917–1921' at the bottom.

Marks:
IPF monogram obliterated by an oval green blob; SPF marks of hammer, sickle and cog plus '1921' in blue overglaze. Dm. 9¼ in. (23.5 cm.)

50

Rudolf F. Vilde

Plate with slogan 'Proletariat of the World Unite' circling the border in Cyrillic letters. The cavetto contains a basket of leaves and flowers plus a large figure 4 made up of leaves and flowers, with the dates 1917–1921 above it. When the plate is held upside-down, one notices that the basket has been superimposed on a bordeaux-coloured word: LIVADIA. It would seem that this plate was originally from a service manufactured for the Imperial summer palace of Livadia in the Crimea. (So far, all similar plates seen by author in public and private collections, within and without the Soviet Union, have had LIVADIA under the basket.)

Marks:
IPF monogram obliterated by an oval green blob; SPF mark of hammer, sickle and cog plus '1921' in blue overglaze. A bordeaux-coloured K in overglaze. (We do not know who K is.) Dm. 9³⁄₁₆ in. (23.4 cm.)

51

Rudolf F. Vilde

Plate with the slogan 'Victory to the Workers – 25th October' circling the grey border. The cavetto contains an elegant wreath of wheat and cornflowers, entwined by a red ribbon, with the emblem of the Soviet Republic in its centre.

Marks:
IPF monogram for Nicholas II, 1913 in green underglaze; SPF mark of hammer, sickle and cog plus '1921' in blue overglaze. No signature. Dm. 9¾ in. (25 cm.)

52

Rudolf F. Vilde (attributed)

Plate with the slogan, 'To All Who are Brave and Young at Heart (put) into their Hands a Book, a Sickle, and a Hammer', circling the border in Cyrillic letters. The cavetto is decorated with an open book, closed books, a hammer and sickle, leaves and grasses. The open book has 'History of the October Revolution Years 1917–1921' written on its pages in Cyrillic. (See note about plate 38 for explanation of the slogan.)

Marks:
IPF monogram for Nicholas II, 1903, semi-obliterated with an oval blob of black paint; SPF mark of hammer, sickle and cog plus '1921', in blue overglaze. Dm. 9½ in. (24 cm.)

53

Rudolf F. Vilde

Plate with slogan 'Long Live the IX Congress' circling the border. The cavetto contains a hammer, part of an iron-red cog and some green leaves. In addition to the slogan, the border contains a stylized sickle and a sunflower superimposed on what seems to be a coat of arms.

Marks:
IPF monogram obliterated with an oval green blob. SPF mark of hammer, sickle and cog plus '1922' in blue overglaze. The mark for SPF artist Alisa R. Golenkina at the very edge of the reverse of the plate, in blue overglaze. Also, pattern number 'No. 27/3' in blue overglaze. Dm. 9¼ in. (23.5 cm.)

53

54

Rudolf F. Vilde

Oval dish with slogan 'We Celebrate Whilst Working – 1 May, 1920'. The centre of the dish contains a multi-coloured bouquet of flowers incorporating a hammer and pliers, the whole entwined by a red and black ribbon. The celebration of May Day, the workers' holiday, was forbidden under the czars.

Marks:

IPF monogram for Nicholas II, 1910 in green underglaze; SPF mark of hammer, sickle and cog plus '1920' in blue overglaze. No signature. Length: 11 in. (28 cm.) Width: 7½ in. (19 cm.)

55

Rudolf F. Vilde

Large dish painted with a worker wielding a sledgehammer and holding a rifle, chasing away a skeletal representation of the Great Reaper (Death). The border is inscribed with Cyrillic letters which read 'In Aid of the Famine-Stricken Population of the Volga Region'.

Marks:

IPF monogram for Alexander III, in green underglaze; SPF mark of hammer, sickle and cog plus '1922' and pattern number '250/19', all in blue overglaze. Inscribed in Cyrillic: 'after the design of R. F. Vilde'. Dm. 13 in. (33 cm.)

56

Rudolf F. Vilde

Plate with slogan, 'Knowledge Lightens Work' in Cyrillic letters. The border is decorated with tools, flowers and leaves. The black part of the trowel's blade covers an heraldic sign.

Marks:

IPF monogram covered with an oval green blob; SPF marks of hammer, sickle and cog plus '1921' in blue overglaze. Dm. 9¼ in. (23.5 cm.)

57

Rudolf F. Vilde (attributed)

Plate with the slogan 'Long Live The VIII Congress Of The Soviets' circling its border in Cyrillic letters. The cavetto is decorated with colourful flowers, wheat ears and leaves.

Marks:

IPF monogram obliterated by an oval green blob; SPF monogram of hammer, sickle and cog plus '1921' in blue overglaze. Dm. 9¾ in. (24.8 cm.)

58

Rudolf F. Vilde

Plate with industrial motifs and agricultural tools, representing workers and peasants. The Cyrillic letters circling the border read 'If your heart yearns for work everything will be reborn'. The letters, though Cyrillic, are designed to look Hebraic. Vilde was Jewish as were many of the revolutionaries.

Marks:

IPF monogram for Nicholas II, 1898 in green underglaze; SPF mark of hammer, sickle and cog, '1921' in blue overglaze; Dm. 9½ in. (24.1 cm.)

54

55

56

57

58

59

Plate based on design by **Pyotr V. Vyechegzhanin**
(Pierre Ino)
Plate known as 'Kommuna' (Commune). (See note to plate no.
60.) A similar plate was left to the National Art Collections Fund
of Great Britain by a former member in 1986. This plate is now
in the Victoria & Albert Museum, London.
Marks:
IPF monogram obliterated by an oval green blob; SPF mark of
hammer, sickle and cog plus '1920' in blue overglaze.
Dm. 8½ in. (21.5 cm.)

60

Plate based on design by **Pyotr V. Vyechegzhanin**
(Pierre Ino)
Plate known as 'RSFSR'. These are the revered initials of the
new Russian Soviet Federated Socialist Republic and were
drawn repeatedly on banners and on porcelain, in gold, in
flowers, or surrounded by flowers, as in this case.

Pyotr Vyéchegzhanin was the son of the graphic artist V.
Levitsky. He had a younger brother, Georgi (1906–50). Both
brothers took their mother, Lydia Vyechegzhanina's surname,
and were later adopted by her second husband, Sergei
Chekhonin. Pyotr emigrated to France with his mother and
Chekhonin in 1928, while Georgi remained in Leningrad. For a
long time the Soviets attributed all Vyechegzhanin plates to
Georgi, but in the late 1960s the Soviet authority Lydia
Andreeva discovered Pyotr's existence and corresponded with
him, since when she attributes all Vyechegzhanin plates to him.
To her he had alleged that he was the sole designer of these
plates but when interviewed in 1987 he claimed to remember
absolutely nothing about the period in question.

If an individual was listed on the worksheet of the SPF, he or
she was entitled to special food coupons, highly desirable in the
difficult years between 1919 and 1922. Pyotr and Georgi were
fifteen and thirteen years old at the time they appear in the
factory's worksheets, and it seems likely that the designs were
actually made by their stepfather, Chekhonin, or, more
probably, by their mother, who was also an artist, and then
attributed to the boys in order to obtain these extra privileges
for them. A few elderly people still living in Leningrad recall
rumours to this effect. Certainly neither boy ever actually
painted porcelain. The plates were all executed by factory
artists, mainly E. N. Potapova.
Marks:
IPF monogram for Nicholas II, 1905 in green underglaze; SPF
mark of hammer, sickle, and cog, plus '1921' in blue overglaze.
Dm. 9⅞ in. (25 cm.)

61

Plate based on design by **Georgi V. Vyechegzhanin**
Plate with large star containing a hammer and sickle, in its
cavetto. The slogan 'Away With the Bourgeoisie, May Capital
Rot' (sic), circles the border in stylized, colourful Cyrillic letters.
(See note to plate no. 60.)
Marks:
IPF monogram for Alexander II, 1880 in green underglaze (this
monogram is rare in Soviet revolutionary porcelain); SPF mark
of hammer, sickle and cog, and '1921' in blue overglaze.
Dm. 8¾ in. (22.2 cm.)

62

Artist Unknown

Large Soviet plate from Dimitrov Factory, 1927, celebrating ten years of the RSFSR's achievements. The centre is painted with a large star inscribed '10 years'. The tips of the star point to the initials composing RSFSR. The lower parts of the star are surrounded by a train, a tractor, broken chains wrapped around an anvil, and a hammer and sickle.
Marks:
Dimitrov Factory mark printed in blue. Dm. 13⅛ in. (33.3 cm.)

63

Artist Unknown

Plate with a portrait of Zinoviev. The Cyrillic letters circling the border proclaim 'Hail to the Fourth Congress of the Third International'.
Marks:
IPF monogram for Nicholas II, 1899 in green underglaze; SPF mark of hammer, sickle and cog, '1922' and '417/7' in blue overglaze. Dm. 9⅜ in. (24 cm.)

62

63

64
Artist Unknown
Teacup and saucer with slogan 'Hail (Long Live) Soviet Power'
on the cup, in Cyrillic. The head of the hammer on both cup and
saucer is painted over an heraldic emblem.
Marks:
IPF monogram for Nicholas II, 1899 on both cup and saucer in
green underglaze; SPF mark of hammer, sickle and cog plus
'1921', on both cup and saucer in blue overglaze.
Height of cup 2⅝ in. (6.5 cm.) Dm. of saucer 5¾ in. (14.5 cm.)

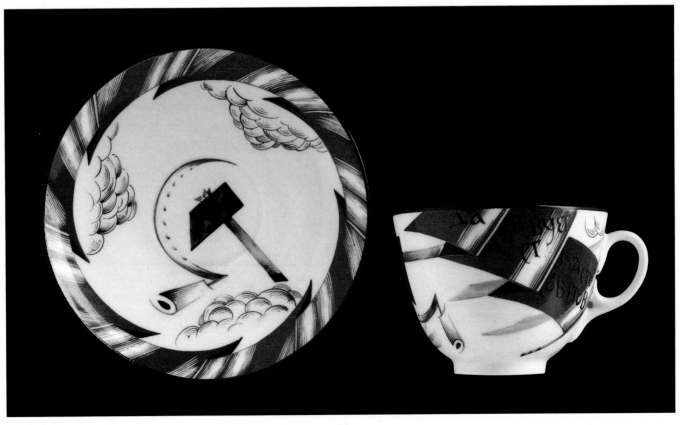

64

Symbolic and Commemorative Pieces

This category includes plates which, though free of slogans, fall within the definition of agitprop because of the message they project about the value of work. They show the symbols and monograms of the new republic and commemorate festivals and anniversaries.

65

Mikhail M. Adamovich

Plate with architectural and agricultural tools circling its border. The cavetto is decorated with a five-pointed red star containing a handplough and a hammer. (This motif appears on many of Adamovich's plates and cups.) The Cyrillic letters for 'AB' which appear at the top of the plate are, of course, the first two letters of the alphabet, seen as the 'tool' for literacy. Including the alphabet amongst the other tools implied that literacy was a necessary tool for building the New Society.
Marks:
IPF monogram for Nicholas II, 1895 in green underglaze; SPF mark of hammer, sickle and cog plus '1921' in blue overglaze. The monogram AB in blue overglaze and the inscription 'after drawing by Adamovich' in Cyrillic, in blue overglaze.
Dm. 9½ in. (24 cm.)

66

Mikhail M. Adamovich

Plate known as 'Red Star'. It has a cobalt-blue border decorated with beautifully designed and executed agricultural and architectural tools and a fishnet containing a fish. All the border decorations are in polished and matt gold. The cavetto, which displays the Adamovich trademark, a red star containing a handplough and a hammer, also shows the monogram of the new republic, RSFSR, in Cyrillic letters, beautifully stylized and executed à la Chekhonin, in tiny gold flowers.
Marks:
IPF monogram obliterated with an oval green blob; SPF mark of hammer, sickle and cog plus '1920' in blue overglaze.
Dm. 9½ in. (24.4 cm.)

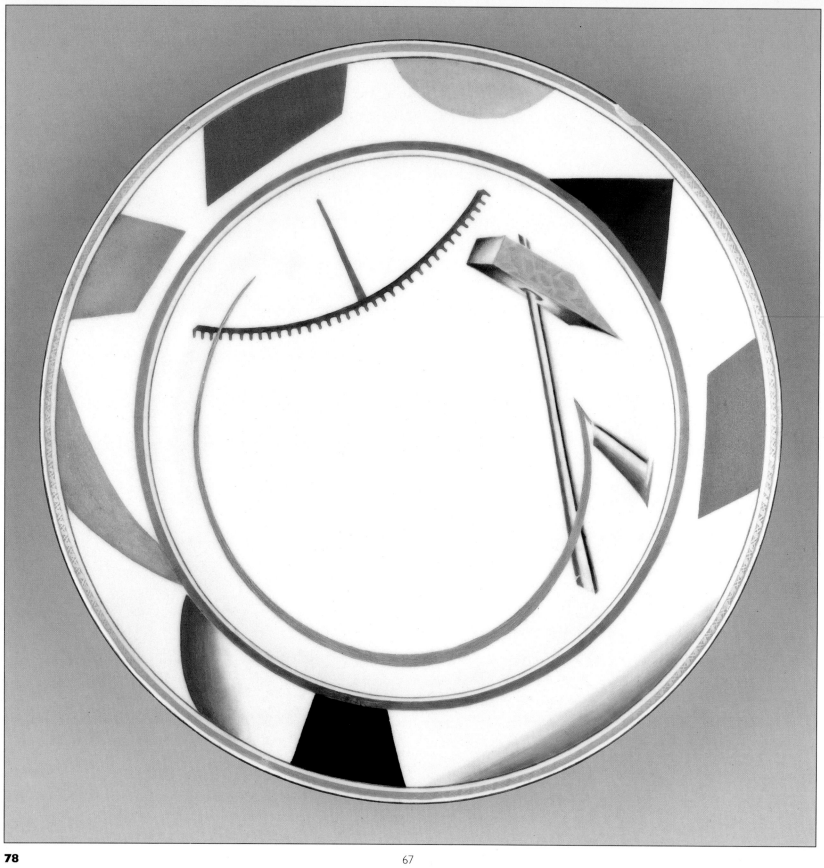

67

67
Sergei V. Chekhonin (Tchekhonine)
Plate known as 'Cubist design with Hammer and Sickle'. The elegant hammer and sickle and the head of a rake occupy the cavetto, while the border is decorated with geometric motifs. This plate shows Chekhonin's genius for adapting and incorporating the most diverse styles into his designs. He even manages to overcome the incompatibility of Cubism and traditionalism, using Cubism very successfully as a means of stylized decoration. The prototype was created in 1919. It was repeated many times for exhibitions in the Soviet Union and abroad. In 1979 an example of this plate was shown at the 'PARIS–MOSCOU 1900–1930' exhibition at the Centre Georges Pompidou, Paris, and was illustrated in the catalogue. Fakes of this plate have been painted in the past ten years.
Marks:
IPF monogram for Alexander III in green underglaze; SPF mark of hammer, sickle and cog plus '1919' and pattern number '281', all in blue overglaze. Dm. $10\frac{1}{8}$ in. (25.8 cm.)

68
Plate based on design by **Sergei V. Chekhonin (Tchekhonine)**
Plate with a ring of colourful fruit and flowers. The black centre contains an elegantly designed gold hammer, sickle and cog.
Marks:
SPF mark of hammer and sickle in green underglaze; '1923' and initials 'V.F.' (Varvara Freze), and '424/24' in blue overglaze. Dm. $9\frac{1}{4}$ in. (23.5 cm.)

69
Sergei V. Chekhonin (Tchekhonine)
Plate known as 'Red Ribbon with Emblem'. Chekhonin, who incorporated the present, the future and the past into his designs, probably took his pleated, encircling ribbon idea from the design of the service for the Knights of the Order of St. Alexander Nevsky, Gardner Factory, commissioned by Catherine II in 1777 and completed in 1780. The cavetto displays the hammer and sickle in gold, together with an ear of wheat. In various SPF documents this plate is referred to as 'Red Cubism'. The prototype was created in 1919. It was repeated many times for exhibitions in the Soviet Union and abroad.
Marks:
IPF obliterated by an oval green blob; SPF mark of hammer and sickle in blue overglaze. Dm. $9\frac{7}{16}$ in. (24 cm.)

68

69

Sergei V. Chekhonin (Tchekhonine)

Plate known as 'Blue Emblem with Flowers'. Elements of the emblem, particularly the sickle, seem to be based on that designed for the SPF by Karev in 1918. It is simply and clearly depicted against a background of small wildflowers: pink roses, pink and yellow clover, little blue flowers, unique in Chekhonin's œuvre in that they are realistically portrayed. Unrealistic, however, but typical of a certain type of popular art in the East, is that all the different flowers issue from a single stem and then spread out, covering the cavetto. The prototype was created in 1918. It was repeated many times for exhibitions in the Soviet Union and abroad.

Marks:

IPF monogram for Nicholas II, 1907 in green underglaze; SPF mark of hammer, sickle and cog, '1918' in blue overglaze.

Dm. $9\frac{5}{8}$ in. (24.5 cm.)

71

Liubov N. Gaush (attributed)

Plate with a portrait of the Decembrist, Gabriil Batenkov in sepia, surrounded by a pleated magenta-coloured banner on which is stated, in Cyrillic letters: 'Batenkov born in 1793 died 1863, held the rank of Lt. Col. in the Army Engineers Corps. He took part in the National Patriotic War [the war against Napoleon]. He spent 20 years in solitary confinement. Came out in 1846 and was sent to supervised residence'. The border is circled by oak leaves. (Oak and laurel wreaths are generally used to crown champions and heroes.)

Marks:

SPF mark of hammer, sickle and cog plus '1920' in blue overglaze. Initial of factory artist, B, in blue overglaze.

Dm. $8\frac{7}{8}$ in. (22.5 cm.)

72

Liubov N. Gaush

Large dish decorated with flowers and looped swags of leaves. Centre contains a golden hammer and sickle.

Marks:

IPF monogram for Alexander III, 1889, in green underglaze; SPF mark of hammer, sickle and cog plus '1921' in blue overglaze. Cyrillic initials for L.G. in blue overglaze.

Dm. $14\frac{1}{2}$ in. (37 cm.)

71

72

73

Zinaida V. Kobyletskaya

Dish, 'Food Products 1921'.
Marks:
IPF monogram for Alexander III 1893 in green underglaze; SPF
mark of hammer, sickle and cog (large and elegantly painted),
plus 'Okt. 20 re 1921' and Kobyletskaya's special mark, all in
blue overglaze. Dm. 13½ in. 34.2 cm.)

74

Zinaida V. Kobyletskaya

Two yellow teacups and saucers with emblems and flowers.
Though not immediately discernible, the cups are decorated
with a sickle and wheelcog in addition to the more noticeable
hammer. They are part of a large tea service.
Marks:
Cup and saucer I SPF mark of hammer, sickle and cog in
green underglaze, no date.
Cup and saucer II SPF mark of hammer and sickle (no cog),
plus 'M', all in blue overglaze. Height of cup 2 in. (5 cm.)
Dm. of saucer 5¾ in. (14.5 cm.)

74

75

75

Maria I. Ivashintsova

Oval platter known as 'The Reaper'.

Marks:

IPF monogram obliterated by an oval green blob; SPF mark of hammer, sickle and cog plus '1920' in blue overglaze.

Length: $23\frac{1}{2}$ in. (59.5 cm.) Width: $11\frac{3}{4}$ in. (30 cm.)

76

Cup and saucer based on design by **Maria V. Lebedeva**

Teacup and saucer showing a mask and a cityscape on the cup, and a factory in the centre of the saucer.

Marks:

Cup IPF monogram for Nicholas II, 1899 in green underglaze; SPF mark of hammer, sickle and cog plus '1921' in blue overglaze; also, 'po riz Lebedevoi' (based on drawing by Lebedeva) and initials 'MK' in Cyrillic, in green overglaze (factory artist Maria Kirilova). Height $2\frac{5}{8}$ in. (6.5 cm.)

Saucer IPF monogram for Nicholas II, 1915 in green underglaze; SPF mark of hammer, sickle and cog plus '1922', pattern number '167/5', and monogram of factory artist E. A. Yakimovskaya, all in blue overglaze. Dm. $5\frac{3}{4}$ in. (14.5 cm.)

77

Maria V. Lebedeva

Large plate with inscription in Cyrillic: 'The Future Has No Fear of Past Horrors'. (Crows and black cats are often the familiars of witches and are therefore associated with sorcery and superstition.)

Marks:

IPF monogram for Nicholas II, 1896 in green underglaze; SPF mark of hammer, sickle and cog plus '1922' in blue overglaze. Lebedeva's monogram, a swan nesting on the letter M ('Lebedev' is the word for swan in Russian) in blue overglaze. Dm. $11\frac{7}{8}$ in. (30.2 cm.)

77

78

Alexandra V. Shchekotikhina-Pototskaya
Plate with cobalt-blue border and a five-pointed gold star,
brightly coloured berries and foliage in the cavetto. The front of
the plate is signed: 'A. Shchekotikhina' in Cyrillic.
Marks:
SPF mark of hammer and sickle in deep-blue overglaze; Signed,
reverse, 'A.Shch., 1920', in deep-blue overglaze.
Dm. 9½ in. (24 cm.)

79

Rudolf F. Vilde (attributed)

Plate with a hammer and sickle in the cavetto and a border decorated with yellow wheat ears and black leaves.

Marks:

IPF monogram obliterated with an oval green blob. SPF mark of hammer, sickle and cog plus '1921' in blue overglaze.

Dm. 9¾ in. (25 cm.)

80

Rudolf V. Vilde (attributed)

Plate entirely covered with flowers and leaves painted with broad brushstrokes, with the date, 1921.

Marks:

IPF monogram covered with an oval green blob; SPF mark of hammer, sickle and cog plus '1921' in blue overglaze.

Dm. 9⅞ in. (25 cm.)

79

80

Design based on a drawing by **Lydia Vyechegzhanina Chekhonin**

Plate with a clown in colourful costume. This commemorates the famous pair of clowns Bim and Bom to whom, for a while, the Soviet authorities granted the right to satirize the shortcomings of the system, thus providing a safety valve for harmlessly releasing pent-up grievances against the regime. The Soviet authority Lydia Andreeva said she had never seen such a plate in the Soviet Union and attributed it to Chekhonin when she was shown photographs of the front and the back in Moscow, March 1988. There used to be a set of ten such plates in London in the thirties. On six of these one could clearly read: 'po riz L.V.' ('based on drawing by L.V.').
Marks:
IPF monogram of Nicholas II, 1915 in green underglaze; SPF mark of hammer, sickle and cog in blue overglaze. Also, pattern number '312/5' in black overglaze, and an unclear inscription in Cyrillic: 'based on drawing by L. . . .'
Dm. 9¼ in. (23.5 cm.)

82
Ekaterina A. Yakimovskaya

Mustard pot with lid, both entirely covered with all sorts of tiny, brightly coloured tools, plus three iron-red stars each surrounded by the Cyrillic letters for RSFSR. A fourth red star decorates the bud finial of the lid. It too is surrounded by the letters RSFSR.

Marks:
SPΓ mark of hammer, sickle and cog plus an indecipherable date in green underglaze under the pot. Signature, 'E. Yakimovskaya', in Cyrillic, plus '1921'. Height $4\frac{1}{2}$ in. (11.5 cm.)

83
N. A. Zander

Plate with star containing a sheaf of wheat and harvesting tools.

Marks:
IPF monogram covered with a black paint patch; SPF mark of hammer, sickle and cog in blue overglaze. Dm. $9\frac{5}{8}$ in. (24.5 cm.)

82

83

Grigorii D. Zimin

Coffee service decorated with forget-me-nots and roundels containing rural scenes, farming implements and a sheaf of wheat with crossed hammer and sickle. Zimin, who had been working at the IPF since 1893, simply went on painting the landscapes with classical architecture and the rural scenes for which he was known, making them topical by inserting a hammer or a factory here and there.

Marks:

Coffeepot IPF monogram for Nicholas II, 1914 in green underglaze; SPF mark of hammer, sickle and cog in blue overglaze; artist's monogram of interlaced Cyrillic 'G' and 'Z' in grey overglaze. Height 5¾ in. (14.5 cm.)

Milk jug IPF monogram for Nicholas II, 1914 in green underglaze; SPF mark of hammer, sickle and cog in blue overglaze plus '1918'. Signed in Cyrillic: 'G. Zimin, 1918' in green overglaze. Height 4¾ in. (12 cm.)

Sugar bowl IPF monogram for Nicholas II, 1914 in green on biscuit; SPF mark of hammer, sickle and cog plus '1918', blue on biscuit; artist's monogram of interlaced Cyrillic 'G' and 'Z' in grey on biscuit. Height 3½ in. (9 cm.)

Coffee can IPF monogram for Nicholas II, 1915 in green on biscuit; SPF mark of hammer, sickle and cog plus '1918', blue on biscuit; artist's monogram of interlaced Cyrillic 'G' and 'Z' in grey on biscuit. Height 2 in. (5 cm.) (The coffeepot, milkpot and sugar bowl all have lids.)

85

Artist Unknown

Plate with scenes of farming over the four seasons of the year, the initials RSFSR (Russian Soviet Federated Socialist Republic), red stars and a gold hammer and sickle (the work tool emblem of the new republic). The scene in the cavetto shows people bringing bags of wheat to a mill or bakery. The sign on the building reads 'A^{oe} O^{oe} KHLEBOPRODUKT' (Shareholders Company of Bread Products) in Cyrillic. The red banner flying on top of the building bears the letters RSFSR in Cyrillic.

The plate is probably propaganda for the New Economic Policy (NEP). The main purpose of NEP, first introduced at the Tenth Party Congress in 1921, was to give the peasants an incentive to produce more, after the disastrous harvest of 1920. Under NEP forcible requisitions of food ceased and the peasants were encouraged to sell their produce on the open market. In towns small private businesses were allowed to spring up.

Marks:
Mark of the Dulevo Factory, 1922 in blue overglaze.
Dm. 9$\frac{3}{4}$ in. (25 cm.)

85

Figurines
These represent characters from the new
Soviet epoch as well as typically Russian figures.

86
Alisa Y. Brusketti-Mitrokhina
The Bourgeoise selling her extra necklaces, petticoats and
teddybear. Prototype created in 1919.
Marks:
SPF mark of hammer, sickle and cog in blue underglaze; '1922'
and '94/2' in blue overglaze. Height 11 in. (28 cm.)
87
Natalya Y. Danko
'At Work'. Self-portrait, mid-1920s, LPF.

86

87

88
Natalya Y. and Elena Y. Danko
Figurine of Anna A. Akhmatova, the great Russian poet who lived in Leningrad and who was a legend in her lifetime. Akhmatova posed for this portrait.
Marks:
SPF mark of hammer, sickle and cog and '1924' in black overglaze plus the double monogram of N. and E. Danko, a Cyrillic 'D' with an 'N' in it and and 'E' under it, all in black overglaze. Height 8⅝ in. (21.8 cm.)

89
Natalya Y. Danko
Factory woman making a speech. The model for the woman was the sculptor's sister Elena Danko, and the figurine is intended as a portrait of her.
Marks:
SPF mark of hammer and sickle in green underglaze plus '1925'. Height 7 in. (17.7 cm.)

90
Natalya Y. Danko (attributed)
Figurine of a young peasant woman in patched clothes with a child seated at her feet. The woman holds a fish in her right hand and another, wrapped in the newspaper *Pravda*, in her left. The child is gnawing at a third fish. The figurine is probably by Natalya Danko.

88

89

90

91

Natalya N. Danko

Sailor with banner. The rope he is holding in his left hand forms
the year – 1921 – at his feet.
Marks:
SPF mark of hammer, sickle and cog in green underglaze. Signed
in Cyrillic with Danko's initials 'ND' impressed in the white base,
plus Maria Briantseva's monogram 'MB' and '1921' in blue
overglaze. Height 7½ in. (19 cm.)

92

Natalya Y. Danko

Lenin inkpot. The inkpot consists of two books, a scroll and a
bust of Lenin standing on them, with a removable inkwell
embedded in the books. The scroll bears a facsimile of Lenin's
two signatures in Cyrillic, in black underglaze. Along the page
edges of the uppermost book runs the slogan 'Proletariat of the
world unite', and on the spine of the lower book, 'Collected
Works of N. Lenin (V. Ulyanov) vol. X', all in Cyrillic and in black
overglaze. There are similar inkpots in numerous public and
private collections in the Soviet Union and the inscriptions vary.
Marks:
SPF mark of hammer, sickle and cog in green underglaze.
Height 6 in. (15.2 cm.)

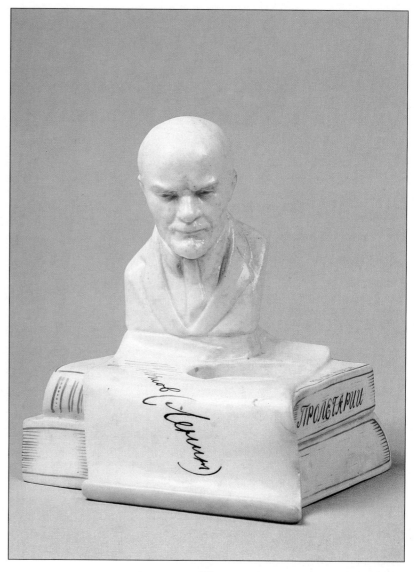

91

92

93
Natalya Y. Danko
Woman sewing banner. Prototype created in 1920. The banner's Cyrillic letters read 'Hail to Soviet Power'.
Marks:
None. Cyrillic letters for 'N' and 'Da', plus '1920' impressed in the white rocks at the base of the figurine. Height 5½ in. (14 cm.)

94
Natalya Y. Danko
Worker holding a rifle. He is standing on the top half of a terrestrial globe inscribed with the first three words of the Internationale.
Marks:
SPF mark of hammer, sickle and cog in green underglaze, plus '1919'. Pattern number, 'No. 91/48' plus special fifth anniversary Narkompros mark in black overglaze. Cyrillic initials 'PA' impressed in paste under the base. Height 6¾ in. (17 cm.)

95
Natalya Y. Danko
'The Red Sailor'. The prototype of this figurine was created in 1918, modelled by Natalya Danko and painted by her sister Elena.
Marks:
SPF mark of hammer, sickle and cog in green underglaze; Cyrillic initials 'PZ' with a line underneath, impressed in paste under the base. Height 7½ in. (19 cm.)

93

94

95

96

96
Natalya Y. Danko
Chess set, 'The Reds and the Whites', prototype created 1922–23 at the State Porcelain Factory.
Height: Red King:
     $4\frac{3}{8}$ in. (11 cm.)
Red Queen:
     $4\frac{1}{4}$ in. (10.7 cm.)
Red Knight:
     $2\frac{15}{16}$ in. (7.4 cm.)
Red Pawn:
     $2\frac{5}{8}$ in. (5.8 cm.)
White King:
     $4\frac{1}{4}$ in. (10.8 cm.)
White Queen:
     4 in. (10.1 cm.)
White Knight:
     $3\frac{1}{8}$ in. (7.9 cm.)
White Pawn:
     $2\frac{5}{16}$ in. (5.9 cm.)

97
Natalya Y. Danko
Newspaper Boy. He is selling the evening edition of the *Krasnaya Gazeta* (Red Gazette).
Marks:
SPF mark of hammer and sickle in blue overglaze.
Height $3\frac{3}{4}$ in. (9.5 cm.)

98
Natalya Y. Danko
'Partisan on the March'. The prototype of this figurine was created in 1919.
Marks:
SPF mark of hammer, sickle and cog in green underglaze, plus special fifth anniversary Narkompros mark in black overglaze. (See note to plate 135.)
Height 8 in. (20 cm.)

Natalya Y. Danko

Group figurine, 'Gypsy fortune teller and elegant young lady'. The streets of Petrograd apparently swarmed with gypsies and nouveau-riche NEP figures in the summer of 1922, when Natalya Danko modelled this group. (Elena Danko posed for the figure of the young lady.)

Marks:

SPF mark of hammer and sickle impressed into paste; 'Made in Russia' in red overglaze. Height $7\frac{9}{16}$ in. (19.2 cm.)

Natalya Y. Danko

Two stevedores unloading sacks of American meal. Prototype created in 1922. One sack is stamped in Roman letters 'AMEPICAIN MEAL U.S.A.' (in Russian 'P' = 'R', hence one misspelling; the 'I' is simply an error). The other sack is stamped in Cyrillic letters 'GOSTORG PETROGRAD RSFSR'. GOSTORG stands for State Trade.

Marks:

SPF mark of hammer, sickle and cog in green underglaze; another hammer, sickle and cog plus '1922' and 'No. 292/3' in blue overglaze. Height $6\frac{1}{2}$ in. (16.5 cm.)

101

Natalya Y. Danko

'Famine'. Group of two emaciated adults and two children
made in 1921, at the time of the severe famine in the lower
Volga region after the disastrous harvest of 1920.
Marks:
None. '1921' incised into base. Height 7$\frac{1}{16}$ in. (18 cm.)

102

Natalya Y. Danko

Turbanned lute player.
Marks:
SPF mark of hammer, sickle and cog in green underglaze. The
special fifth anniversary Narkompros mark (see note to plate
135), '447/21' and a monogram composed of the letters 'E' and
'M' are all in black overglaze. Height 5 in. (12.5 cm.)

101

102

103

Elena Y. Danko

Turkic Girl reading. Prototype created in 1921. In September 1919, Zinoviev presided over the Congress of the Peoples of the East in Baku. This delightful figurine shows a bare-breasted and veiled girl reading a newspaper with the Cyrillic headline 'Congress of the Peoples of the East' and a silhouette of Zinoviev's head occupying the centre of the page. According to an old friend of the Danko family, still living in Leningrad, the model for the Turkic girl was Natalya Danko. She looked like a gypsy and enjoyed oriental disguises.

Marks:

SPF mark of hammer and sickle in green underglaze; dated '1923' and inscribed '220/18' in blue overglaze.

Height 4½ in. (11.5 cm.)

104

P. Kamensky

Peasant sowing. This is from a series of over one hundred figurines called 'Types of Russia', which was first created by the Imperial Factory in the eighteenth century and recreated in 1908–10 for the Ethnographic Museum, St. Petersburg, by P. Kamensky. The figurines made for the museum were about fourteen inches high. Smaller figurines, about seven inches high were also made. They were given as presents during the czarist period and, later, were made for sale. The peasant is labelled as 'Veliki Ross iz Rizanyi', or 'the Russian man from Ryazan'.

Marks:

'1917', in green overglaze. This mark is extremely rare as it was used only in March and April 1917, immediately after the February 1917 Revolution. Height 7 in. (17.7 cm.)

105

Vasilii V. Kuznetsov

'The Red Guard'. Prototype created in 1918. This is the first Soviet sculpture in porcelain representing a man of the new epoch, the defender of the people's state.

Marks:

SPF mark of hammer and sickle in green underglaze. Signature of factory artist, 'N. Daladugin', in Cyrillic, in black underglaze.

Height 8¼ in. (21 cm.)

106

Figurine, possibly modelled by

Vasilii V. Kuznetsov

after a design by

Boris M. Kustodiev

Red Army soldier holding a rifle and wearing a white fur-lined greatcoat.

Marks:

SPF mark of hammer and sickle in blue overglaze.

Height 7½ in. (19 cm.)

105

106

107

Vasilii V. Kuznetsov

Man with large sturgeon. This belongs to the 'Signs of the Zodiac' series, designed by Kuznetsov.
Marks:
SPF marks of hammer, sickle and cog, special fifth anniversary Narkompros mark plus '99/13' in black overglaze.
Height 6⅞ in. (17.7 cm.)

108

Alexander T. Matveev

Figurine of a seated, naked woman holding a green basin. Prototype created in 1923. Matveev was a well-known Russian sculptor and there was much excitement at the State Porcelain Factory when Chekhonin persuaded him to have six small models of nude women turned into porcelain figurines, instead of being first cast in bronze. They made an impact as a new approach to the possibilities of porcelain. All of them had a monumental quality.
Marks:
SPF mark of hammer, sickle and cog in blue overglaze; signed in Cyrillic, 'sculptor A. T. Matveev', plus '1926' and the Cyrillic letter for 'g', which stands for year. Height 6 in. (15 cm.)

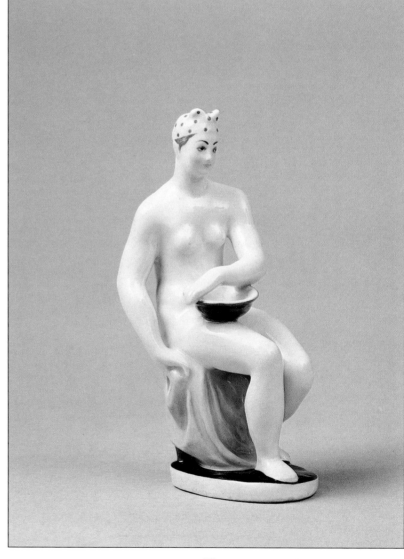

107

108

109
Sergei V. Chekhonin (Tchekhonine)
Figurine of seated, naked woman putting on a slipper. The original was created at the SPF by Matveev in 1923. This figurine was made two years later at the Volkhov Factory, and painted by Chekhonin.
Marks:
Volkhov monogram (designed by Chekhonin) and '1925' plus 'Volkhov' and 'sculptor A. T. Matveev', all in Cyrillic, in Chekhonin's handwriting, on the back rim of the base.
Height 6¼ in. (16 cm.)

110
Yakov A. Trupiansky
Figurine of Feodor Chaliapin as Boris Godunov. Prototype created in 1922.
Marks:
SPF mark has been scratched out underneath base. Trupiansky's signature, in Cyrillic, plus '1922' are impressed in the rim of the base. Height 11 in. (28 cm.)

109

110

Traditional Themes

These represent scenes and subjects of eternal Russia – rural life, motherhood, peasants and fishermen.

Mikhail M. Adamovich

Saucer completely covered with a leafy bouquet of colourful flowers in a polished and matt gold vase. (In 1988 the State Museum of Ceramics at Kuskovo acquired an entire tea service with this pattern from Adamovich's grandchildren.)

The curator at Kuskovo did not know for sure by whom the tea service was until she saw a photograph of the back of the Nicholas Lynn saucer, with the inscription: 'based on design by Adamovich'. The design is totally atypical of his work.
Marks:
IPF monogram for Alexander III, 1889 in green underglaze; SPF mark of hammer, sickle and cog plus '1922' in blue overglaze. 'Po riz Adamovicha' (based on drawing by Adamovich), in blue overglaze, in Cyrillic letters. Also pattern number 272/3 in blue overglaze. Dm. $5\frac{3}{4}$ in. (14.5 cm.)

Mikhail M. Adamovich

Coffee can and saucer decorated with rural scenes and the tools for harvesting and fishing.
Marks:
Cup IPF monogram for Alexander III, 1889 in green underglaze; SPF mark of hammer, sickle and cog plus '1922', in blue overglaze. Also, 'based on design by Adamovich', in Cyrillic, and the monogram of factory artist E. A. Yakimovskaya, plus pattern number 'N 139/5', all in blue overglaze. Height: $2\frac{3}{4}$ in. (7 cm.)
Saucer Provisional Government mark plus '1917' in green underglaze (see note on plate 19 for description of this mark); SPF mark of hammer, sickle and cog plus '1922' in blue overglaze. Also the monogram of E. A. Yakimovskaya, 'based on design by Adamovich' in Cyrillic and pattern number 'N 139/5', all in blue overglaze. Dm. $5\frac{1}{2}$ in. (14 cm.)

113

Dish based on design by **Léon Bakst (Rozenberg, Lev Samoilovich)**

Shaped, oval dish finely painted in glowing, enamelled colours with Nijinsky in the role of Iskander in Diaghilev's projected ballet 'La Péri' (1911). The design is after the original costume design by Bakst now in the Metropolitan Museum, New York. This unique porcelain dish was decorated at the Lomonosov Porcelain Factory in 1925, probably as a tribute to Bakst who had died the previous year. It was bought and taken to Sweden by Alexandra Kollontai, Soviet Ambassador to Sweden from 1930 to 1945. There are several other oval dishes at the LPF Museum decorated with dancers wearing gorgeous costumes based on designs by Bakst.

Marks:

IPF monogram for Alexander III, 1893 in green underglaze; LPF mark of hammer, sickle and cog plus '1925' in black overglaze.

Length: $15\frac{1}{4}$ in. (40 cm.) Width: $11\frac{1}{2}$ in. (29.3 cm.)

113

114

Sergei V. Chekhonin (Tchekhonine)
Plate, coffee can and saucer with cobalt-blue borders decorated with golden and oxidized silver flowers, plus white and red flowers and green leaves. This plate and matching cup and saucer, in Chekhonin's Empire style, belonged to Chekhonin himself and came out of the Soviet Union with him when he emigrated to France.
Marks:
Plate IPF monogram for Nicholas II, 1898 in green underglaze; SPF mark of hammer, sickle and cog in gold overglaze plus initials 'S.Ch.' in Cyrillic and '1921' all in gold overglaze, as well as the monogram, RSFSR, exquisitely designed and painted by Chekhonin, in green, red and gold Cyrillic letters. (RSFSR stands for Russian Soviet Federated Socialist Republic.) Dm. 9½ in. (24 cm.)
Cup IPF monogram for Nicholas II, 1905 in green underglaze; SPF mark of hammer, sickle and cog plus '1922'; also initials 'S.Ch.' as well as 'Sergei Chekhonin' in Cyrillic, all in blood-red overglaze. Height 3 in. (7.5 cm.)
Saucer IPF monogram for Nicholas II, 1905 in green underglaze; SPF monogram of hammer, sickle and cog plus '1922'; also initials 'S.Ch.' in Cyrillic, all in blood-red overglaze. Dm. 6 in. (15.5 cm.)

115

Sergei V. Chekhonin (Tchekhonine)

Teacup and saucer decorated with a silhouette bust of Chekhonin's wife, Lydia S. Vyechegzhanina, surrounded by an oval garland of flowers and leaves. The cup is signed under the silhouette, in Cyrillic: 'Sergei Chekhonin, 1923'. This cup and saucer are unique. They came out of the Soviet Union with Chekhonin in 1928.

Marks:

Cup IPF monogram for Alexander III, 1892 in green underglaze; no SPF mark. Height 3 in. (7.5 cm.)
Saucer IPF monogram for Alexander III, 1893 in green underglaze; SPF mark of hammer, sickle and cog plus '1922' in blue overglaze. Dm. $6\frac{1}{4}$ in. (16 cm.)

116

Plate based on design by **Sergei V. Chekhonin (Tchekhonine)**

Plate with white cavetto and a border decorated with elegant, stylized flowers and leaves, plus gilded inner and outer rim. (When shown a colour photograph of this plate Soviet authority Lydia Andreeva said that it was probably based on a design by Chekhonin for one of the new embassy services in the twenties.)

Marks:

IPF monogram for Nicholas II, 1907 in green underglaze; SPF mark of hammer, sickle and cog plus '1921' in blue overglaze. Dm. $9\frac{9}{16}$ in. (24.5 cm.)

115

116

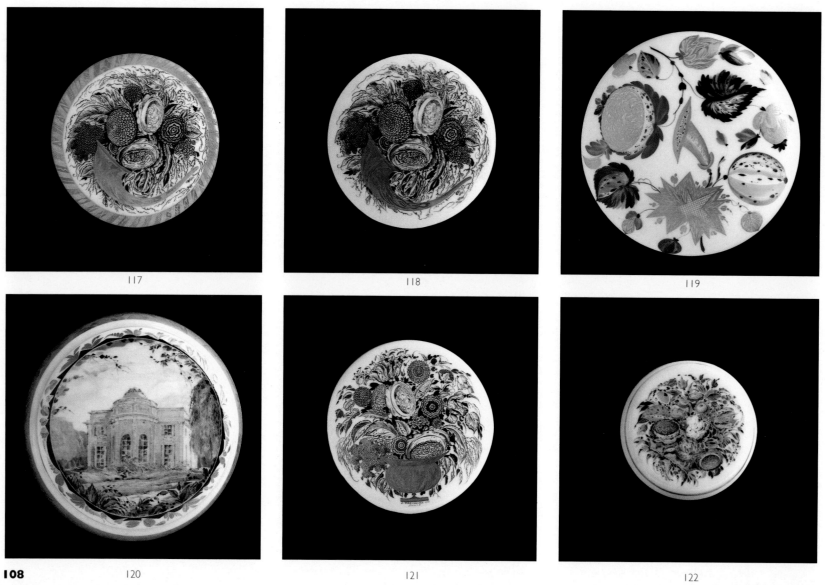

117

118

119

120

121

122

Sergei V. Chekhonin (Tchekhonine)

117

I Circular porcelain powder container with lid. The lid is decorated with a golden cornucopia from which issue delicately etched black flowers, typical of Chekhonin. The lid is signed in Cyrillic, 'Sergei Chekhonin, 1922' in black overglaze.
Marks:
Lid None.
Bottom Provisional Government mark of crownless, double-headed eagle within a hyphenated circle, plus 1917, all in green underglaze. Signature 'Sergei Chekhonin' in black overglaze, in swirling, decorative, Cyrillic letters. Dm. $2\frac{1}{2}$ in. (6.5 cm.)

118

II Circular porcelain powder container with lid. The lid is decorated with a mass of delicately etched black flowers.
Marks:
Lid None.
Bottom SPF mark of hammer, sickle and cog plus '1922' and '295/1' in grey on biscuit. Dm. $3\frac{1}{8}$ in. (8 cm.)

Sergei V. Chekhonin (Tchekhonine)

Four Sèvres porcelain containers, beautifully decorated by Chekhonin during his first year in Paris. He had hoped that Sèvres would purchase his prototypes in order to produce multiples but was disappointed. (The Sèvres mark was obliterated by Sèvres before releasing the items for decoration to someone outside the factory.) After moving to Paris, Chekhonin stopped signing his work in Cyrillic and usually signed 'Serge Tchekhonine' in Roman letters. He had studied gilding and goldsmithing techniques and was very proud of his expertise. Therefore he occasionally made a point of signing his superb goldwork within the gold. Two of these containers are so signed.

119

I Large, circular porcelain container, the lid decorated with flowers and leaves and signed 'S. Tchekhonine, 1928, Paris'. Dm. $5\frac{1}{2}$ in. (14.2 cm.)

120

II Circular porcelain powder container, the lid decorated with the pavilion of Bagatelle. (Chekhonin's pencil drawing for the design is inside the container.) The bottom is encircled by a wide band of scratched gold, decorated with a design of leaves and flowers. The lid is signed: 'S. Tchekhonine, Paris, 1928', in black within the greenery, and 'Serge Tchekhonine' is etched into the gold band of the bottom part. Dm. $4\frac{1}{4}$ in. (11 cm.)

121

III Circular porcelain container with lid decorated with a golden pedestal vase full of stylized black and red flowers. The bottom part is encircled by a gold band etched with Suprematist motifs. The lid is signed: 'S. Tchekhonine, 1928, Paris', in black. 'Serge Tchekhonine, 1928' is etched into the encircling gold band. Dm. $3\frac{1}{2}$ in. (9 cm.)

122

IV Small, circular porcelain pillbox which is decorated with a basket of delicate flowers. Signature, 'S. Tchekhonine, Paris, 1928', on the lid, amongst leaves under the basket. Dm. $2\frac{1}{4}$ in. (5.5 cm.)

Sergei V. Chekhonin (Tchekhonine)

Teapot decorated on front side with flowers of various colours, green leaves and a grey melon-like shape. The back is decorated with a large, blue rose-shaped flower. This side is signed 'S. Chekhonin, 1923', plus Volkhov monogram and 'Volkhov' all in Cyrillic, in green underglaze. See note to no. 141.
Marks:
Nothing on bottom of teapot. Height: $6\frac{1}{2}$ in. (16.5 cm.)

124

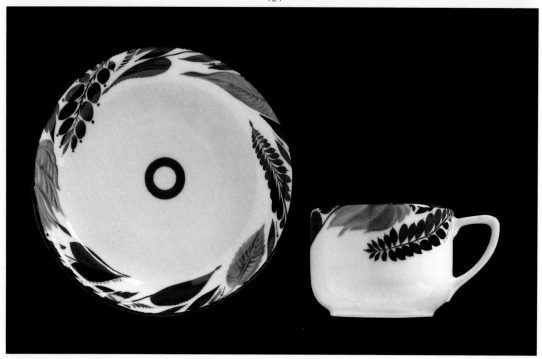

124

Sergei V. Chekhonin (Tchekhonine)

Teacup and saucer decorated by Chekhonin as a nameday present for his wife Lydia. The centre of the saucer contains a beautiful Cyrillic 'L' composed of tiny, multi-coloured and gold flowers. Chekhonin's decoration for this cup and saucer served as a prototype for a series later produced by the Lomonosov Porcelain Factory, minus the 'L'. Both cup and saucer are signed 'Sergei Chekhonin, 1924', in Cyrillic.

Marks:

Cup The Volkhov Factory monogram, 1924, 'Volkhov' and initials 'S.Ch.', all in Cyrillic, in black overglaze.
Height $2\frac{3}{16}$ in. (5.5 cm.)

Saucer The Volkhov Factory monogram, 1924, 'Volkhov' plus 'Sergei Chekhonin', all in Cyrillic, in black overglaze.
Dm. $5\frac{1}{2}$ in. (13.8 cm.)

125

Sergei V. Chekhonin (Tchekhonine)

Ceramic teacup and saucer decorated with leaves and a circle in the middle of the saucer. Signed 'S. Chekhonin, 1923' in Cyrillic on both cup and saucer in black overglaze.

Marks:

Cup The Volkhov Factory monogram plus 'Volkhov' in Cyrillic and '1923', all in black overglaze, plus the Cyrillic initials 'S.Ch.'
Height $2\frac{1}{8}$ in. (5.5 cm.)

Saucer The Volkhov Factory monogram plus 'Volkhov' in Cyrillic and '1923', plus the Cyrillic initials 'S.Ch.', all in black overglaze. Dm. $5\frac{1}{2}$ in. (14 cm.)

Between 1923 and 1925, Chekhonin directed artistic work at the Volkhov Factory near Novgorod. This cup and saucer seem to be unique. Chekhonin took them with him when he emigrated to France in 1928.

126

Sergei V. Chekhonin (Tchekhonine)
Pencil and watercolour drawings for the decoration of two cups.
Cup I Drawing for a cup with gold rim, foot and handle and exquisitely designed Cyrillic initials 'V M' in tiny, multi-coloured flowers reminiscent of those one sees on eighteenth-century Sèvres porcelain. Signed in pencil: 'Sergei 1919 Chekhonin', in Cyrillic. Height: $2\frac{5}{8}$ in. (5.9 cm.)
Cup II Drawing for a cup with gold rim, foot and handle and Cyrillic initials 'B M M' in tiny, multi-coloured flowers. Signed in pencil: 'Sergei 1921 Chekhonin' in Cyrillic. Height: $2\frac{5}{8}$ in. (5.9 cm.)
127
Sergei V. Chekhonin (Tchekhonine)
Empire-style coffee cup painted cobalt blue and decorated with a pedestal vase containing a multi-coloured bouquet and surrounded by a gold wreath. Gold flowers and green leaves are strewn all over the cup. Signature in Cyrillic under the bouquet: 'S. Chekhonin, 1922'.
Marks:
SPF mark of hammer, sickle and cog in blue overglaze, date illegible. Height 3 in. (7.5 cm.)

128

Varvara P. Freze

Large plate entirely covered with colourful flowers emerging from a tiny brown basket, plus a large butterfly.

Marks:

IPF monogram for Nicholas II, 1913 in green underglaze; SPF mark of hammer, sickle and cog plus '1922' in blue overglaze; also pattern number 'N. 170' in blue overglaze. 'B. Freze', in Cyrillic, on reverse in blue overglaze. Dm. 12¼ in. (31 cm.)

129

Cup and saucer, based on a design by S. V. Chekhonin, by

Varvara P. Freze

Cup decorated with a large, scratched gold, puce and white flower and elegant black, gold and green leaves.

Marks:

Cup SPF mark of hammer, sickle and cog in green underglaze; in Cyrillic, 'V. Freze based on design by S. V. Chekhonin', plus '1926' in black overglaze. Height 2 in. (5 cm.)

Saucer SPF mark of hammer, sickle and cog in green underglaze. Dm. 5¾ in. (14.5 cm.)

130

Natalya A. Girshfeld

Plate with colourful berries and vegetables in the border and a jagged black design around the cavetto.

Marks:

IPF monogram obliterated by a dark green diamond-shaped blob; SPF mark of hammer, sickle and cog, and initials 'N.G.' in Cyrillic, all in blue overglaze. Dm. 9⅜ in. (23.7 cm.)

128

129

Maria I. Ivashintsova

Teacup and saucer decorated with boldy designed flowers and triangular motifs which continue over the rims. Ivashintsova's painting on porcelain was distinguished by an especially broad brushstroke.

Marks:

Cup IPF monogram obliterated by an oval green blob; SPF mark of hammer, sickle and cog plus '1919' in blue overglaze. Height: 3 in. (7.5 cm.)

Saucer IPF monogram obliterated by a dark green oval patch; SPF mark of hammer, sickle and cog plus '1919' in blue overglaze. Dm. 6¼ in. (16 cm.)

Zinaida V. Kobyletskaya

Tea service known as 'Flowers'. It is made of very thin porcelain. The tray is extremely light. Lydia Andreeva thinks that this tea service may have been painted by Kobyletskaya for her own use. She has never seen another either in the Soviet Union or elsewhere.

Marks:

Tray IPF monogram for Alexander II, 1880 in green underglaze; SPF mark of hammer, sickle and cog, 1922, Z. Kobyletskaya's signature and monogram in blue overglaze; also, 'G.O.' and 'N.259/1' in blue overglaze.

Teapot IPF monogram for Alexander II (blurred), 1872 in green underglaze; the rest same as on the tray. Height 6 in. (15.2 cm.)

Milk jug IPF monogram for Alexander III, 1888 in green underglaze; the rest same as on the tray, minus Kobyletskaya's signature. Height 4 in. (10 cm.)

Sugarbowl IPF monogram for Nicholas II, 1909 in green underglaze; SPF mark of hammer, sickle and cog plus '1922', '259/1' and Kobyletskaya's monogram in blue overglaze. Height 4¾ in. (12 cm.)

Cup I IPF monogram for Alexander III, 1892 in green underglaze; SPF mark of hammer, sickle and cog plus '1922', Kobyletskaya's monogram and pattern number '259', all in blue overglaze. Height: 2⅛ in. (5⅜ cm.)

Cup II IPF monogram for Alexander III, 1892 (unclear) in green underglaze; SPF mark of hammer, sickle and cog plus '1922', Kobyletskaya's monogram and 'N.259/1', all in blue overglaze. Height same as above.

Saucer I IPF monogram for Alexander III, 1894 (unclear) in green underglaze; the rest same as on tray except that, like Cup I, it only bears the pattern number '259' with no slash or second number. Dm. 5½ in. (14 cm.)

Saucer II IPF monogram for Nicholas II, 1902 in green underglaze; the rest same as on the tray. Dm. same as above.

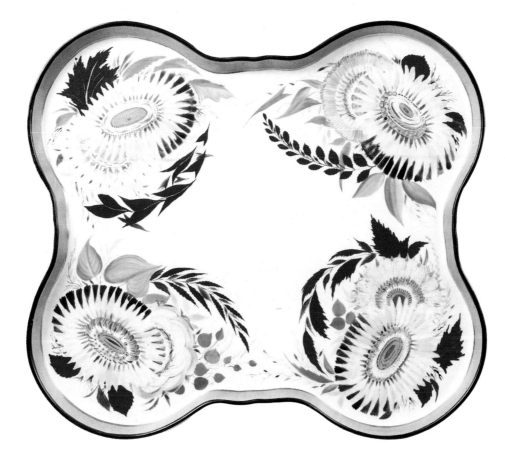

132

133
Vladimir S. Mosyagin
Large plate decorated with an architectural fantasy.
Marks:
IPF monogram for Alexander III, 1893 in green underglaze; SPF mark of hammer, sickle and cog in blue overglaze; pattern number 'N.332/1', trefoil mark of factory artist Vasilii P. Timorev followed by '22.V' and 'po.B.M.' in Cyrillic (based on sketch by V.M.), all in blue overglaze. Dm. 12¼ in. (31 cm.)

134
Valentin S. Shcherbakov (attributed)
Plate decorated with a small log cabin surrounded by pine trees.
Marks:
IPF monogram obliterated by green diamond-shaped patch; SPF mark of hammer, sickle and cog plus '1921' in blue overglaze. Initials 'O A' (unidentified) on reverse. Dm. 8¾ in. (22 cm.)

135
Alexandra V. Shchekotikhina-Pototskaya
Plate known as 'Motherhood'. This is a famous plate which was repeated time and again both by Shchekotikhina herself and by factory artists. One finds it in numerous public and private collections.
Marks:
IPF monogram for Nicholas II, 1902 or 1908 (unclear) in green underglaze; SPF special jubilee mark produced for Fifth Anniversary of the People's Commissariat for Public Education. Hence the initials KHP in black overglaze. (The monogram was designed by Chekhonin.) This mark commemorates the fact that the SPF was placed under the authority of the KHP and involved in their propaganda campaign. 'Po riz A. Shchekotikhinoi' in Cyrillic (based on design by A. Shchekotikhina), in black overglaze. Also initials 'M.K.' (initials of factory artist Maria Petrovna Kirilova), in black overglaze. Dm. 10½ in. (26.7 cm.)

133

134

136

Ekaterina A. Yakimovskaya

Plate with a peasant girl carrying a yoke and two buckets.
Marks:
IPF monogram for Nicholas II, 1898 in green underglaze; SPF
mark of hammer, sickle and cog plus '1922' in blue overglaze.
Pattern number 'N 69/7' and monogram of factory artist E. A.
Yakimovskaya, both in blue overglaze. Dm. 9½ in. (24.2 cm.)

137

Aleksei V. Vorobevsky

Small teapot decorated with lace-like leafy motifs around the
upper part of the body and on the lid. Vorobevsky (b. 1906) is
one of the few artists from the first decade of the SPF who is
still alive and decorating porcelain today.
Marks:
LPF mark of hammer, sickle and cog in green underglaze.
Height 3½ in. (9 cm.)

136

137

138
Artist unknown

Oval platter, 'The Swing'.

Marks:

IPF monogram for Nicholas II, 1908 in green underglaze; SPF mark of hammer, sickle and cog plus '1921', in blue overglaze.

Length: 17 in. (44 cm.) Width: 12¼ in. (31 cm.)

139

Artist unknown, probably Bazilka N. Radonich

Teapot, sugar bowl with lid and two teacups decorated with coral-red and gold stylized leaves and flowers.

Marks:

Teapot IPF monogram for Nicholas II, 1913 in green underglaze; SPF mark of hammer, sickle and cog, plus '1923' (blurred) and pattern number 'N 413/1' in blue overglaze.

Height 5½ in. (14 cm.)

Sugar bowl IPF monogram for Nicholas II, 1899 in green underglaze; SPF mark of hammer, sickle and cog, date '1923', plus pattern number 'N 413/1' in blue overglaze.

Height 4¾ in. (12 cm.)

Teacups Provisional Government Period mark of crownless, double-headed eagle within a hypenated circle, plus date, '1917', all in green underglaze; SPF mark of hammer, sickle and cog, '1923', and pattern number 'N 413/1' on one cup and 'N 413/11' on the other, all in blue overglaze.

Height 2¼ in. (5.5 cm.)

All four items have the Cyrillic initial for 'B' in blue overglaze on reverse. Although several artists signed with this initial, in this case the 'B' is probably for Bazilka. (See page listing monograms and initials of porcelain artists.)

138

139

Russian Folklore

Subjects drawn from folklore – the Firebird, Sadko, wood spirits and scenes from the tales of Pushkin.

Sergei V. Chekhonin (Tchekhonine)
Teacup and saucer decorated with a black mask sprouting roots and leaves and a black and gold flower.
Marks:
Cup IPF monogram for Alexander III, '744894' in green underglaze; SPF mark of hammer, sickle and cog plus '1922' in blue overglaze. Height 3 in. (7.5 cm.)
Saucer Same marks as above. Dm. 6¼ in. (16 cm.)

141

Sergei V. Chekhonin (Tchekhonine)
Teapot known as 'Sirin' because it is decorated on its front side with the fabled bird-woman of Russian folklore of this name. On the back it is decorated with a large melon-shaped fruit of various colours. It has been signed on both sides 'S. Chekhonin, 1923' in Cyrillic, in black overglaze. This teapot belonged to Chekhonin and he brought it out of the Soviet Union with him when he emigrated. From 1923 to 1925, Chekhonin directed the artistic work at the Volkhov Factory near Novgorod.
Marks:
Teapot bottom: Volkhov monogram, '1923', plus word 'Volkhov' in Cyrillic, in black overglaze, all by Chekhonin.
Lid bottom: Volkhov monogram plus '1923' and the word 'Volkhov' in Cyrillic, all in black overglaze, all by Chekhonin. Height 5½ in. (14 cm.)

140

141

142

Zinaida V. Kobyletskaya

Large dish known as the 'City of Kitez'. It depicts the legendary
city, encircled by a moat, within an octagonal gold frame.

Marks:

IPF monogram for Alexander III, 1893 in green underglaze; SPF
mark of hammer, sickle and cog plus '1922' in blue overglaze,
and the pattern number '268/2' in black overglaze.

Dm. 12 in. (30.5 cm.)

142

143

Georgi I. Narbut

Rectangular dish decorated with a silhouette illustrating Hans Christian Andersen's fairytale 'The Nightingale'. Narbut was a professor at the Academy of Arts in Kiev. At the suggestion of Chekhonin his silhouette graphics were used on a series of ceramics intended for export, produced by the State Porcelain Factory in 1920–23. (Andersen was very fond of cutting silhouettes and illustrated many of his stories with his own work. These can be seen at the Hans Andersen Museum at Odense, Denmark – one wonders if Narbut knew about Andersen's silhouettes.)

Marks:

IPF monogram for Nicholas II, 1913 in green on biscuit; SPF mark of hammer, sickle and cog plus '1922', Cyrillic initials 'E.Ya.' (Ekaterina Yakimovskaya) plus 'Po riz. Narbuta' (based on a design by Narbut), and pattern number 'N.191/2', all in blue on biscuit. Length 10 in. (25.5 cm.) Width 7 in. (17.7 cm.)

144

Yelizaveta B. Rozendorf (based on a design by Chekhonin)

Oval platter known as 'Firebird'.

Marks:

IPF monogram for Alexander II in green underglaze (rare in Soviet revolutionary porcelain); SPF mark of hammer, sickle and cog plus '1925', beautifully painted in blue overglaze.

Length: 14 in. (35.5 cm.) Width: 11½ in. (29 cm.)

145

Cup, saucer and plate based on designs by **Alexandra V. Shchekotikhina-Pototskaya**

Cup, saucer and plate decorated with Sun and Moon faces, stars and eyes. This was a favourite motif of Shchekotikhina-Pototskaya.

Marks:

Cup IPF monogram obliterated by an oval green blob; SPF mark of hammer, sickle and cog plus '1922' in blue overglaze. Also pattern number '26/1' in black overglaze.
Height 3 in. (7.5 cm.)

Saucer IPF monogram obliterated by an oval green blob; SPF mark of hammer, sickle and cog plus '1922' in blue overglaze. Also pattern number '26/1' in black overglaze.
Dm. 6¼ in. (15.8 cm.)

Plate IPF monogram for Nicholas II, 1910 in green underglaze (diamond-shaped green paint patch covers 'N II' but the '1910' is uncovered); SPF mark of hammer, sickle and cog plus '1919' in blue overglaze. Letters 'OAA' in bluish-green overglaze on rim of foot, reverse of plate. Dm. 7⅛ in. (18 cm.)

145

146

Cup and saucer based on a design by **Alexandra V. Shchekotikhina-Pototskaya**

Teacup and saucer decorated with a story from 'Skasku Pushkina' (Tales of Pushkin).

Marks:

Cup IPF monogram for Nicholas II, 1899 in green underglaze; SPF mark of hammer, sickle and cog plus '1922' and pattern number '93/3', all in blue overglaze. Height 2½ in. (6.5 cm.)

Saucer IPF monogram for Nicholas II, 1898 in green underglaze; SPF mark of hammer, sickle and cog plus '1922', in blue overglaze. Also the monogram of V. F. Rukavishnikova (a factory artist) in blue overglaze. Dm. 6¼ in. (15.8 cm.)

147

Artist unknown, possibly Vasilii V. Kuznetsov

A mug, the front part of which is modelled and painted with the face of an old man (possibly the traditional Old Man of the Forest). The sides and back of the mug and parts of the face are decorated with plants, flowers and berries. The handle is shaped and painted to simulate a silver birch branch.

This is a particularly detailed piece of modelling and painting. It exudes the artist's affection for the Russian birchwoods in summer.

Marks:

SPF mark of hammer, sickle and cog plus '1922' and the pattern number 'N 404/3', all in blue overglaze. Height 4 in. (10 cm.)

148

Artist Unknown (unclear signature appears to read 'R. Telkina')

Plate known as 'Sadko'. Sadko, a singer from Novgorod, is the hero of the much-loved opera/ballet by Rimsky-Korsakov. He is shown in an underwater cavern, wearing a medieval Russian costume and playing a golden gusli. He is surrounded by shells, seaweed, fish, a starfish and a dish containing a jug and fruit.

Marks:

IPF monogram for Nicholas II, 1908 in green underglaze; SPF marks and date scratched out. Pattern number '380/2' in mauve overglaze. Signature: 'R. Telkina' (unclear) in mauve overglaze plus, in Cyrillic, 'painted by' – a few letters are missing – initials G.Z. (factory artist G. Zimin). Dm. 10⅜ in. (26.3 cm.)

149

Artist Unknown

Plate containing a colourful walled city divided by a river spanned by a bridge. In the background is an immense black fish with green wings, and in the foreground a small, yellow boat. This is probably an episode from one of the numerous Russian folk tales involving huge, magical fish, or monstrous whales. On some plates and cups a fish is breaking through a net, representing the Revolution tearing away the cobwebs of prejudice.

Marks:

IPF monogram for Nicholas II, 1908 in green underglaze; SPF mark of hammer, sickle and cog in blue overglaze. The Cyrillic initials PR in blue overglaze, unidentified as yet. Also, pattern number 'N. 565' in blue overglaze. Dm. 9⅜ in. (23.8 cm.)

148

149

The Avant Garde

Cubist, Suprematist and abstract pieces.

150
Ilia G. Chashnik
Plate with black Suprematist design and a wide black border.
Marks:
IPF monogram for Alexander III, 1889 in green underglaze; SPF mark of hammer and sickle, SUPREMATISM, N 474, a black square within a square and the signature 'Il. Chashnik,' all in Cyrillic and in black overglaze. LPF inventory letters and number 3127.

151
Ilia G. Chashnik
Mustard pot with lid, both decorated with Suprematist designs.
Marks:
The word 'SUPREMATISM', N 474, a black square within a square, and the signature, 'Il. Chashnik', all in Cyrillic in black overglaze. LPF inventory letters and the number, 3131.
Height: 4½ in. (11.5 cm.)

152
Ilia G. Chashnik
Plate with Suprematist design in the cavetto, encircled by a black ring.
Marks:
IPF monogram for Nicholas II, 1912 in green underglaze; SPF mark of hammer, sickle and cog, and '1923' in blue overglaze. 'I. CHASHNIK', printed in capital Cyrillic letters, in black overglaze. The word 'SUPREMATISM' in printed, capital Cyrillic letters under Chashnik's signature, also in black overglaze. Also a filled-out red square within a black square in black overglaze, plus pattern number 'No.453' in black overglaze. Dm. 9⅜ in. (23.8 cm.)

153
Nikolai M. Suetin
Plate with orange, black and magenta Suprematist design.
Marks:
IPF monogram for Nicholas II, 1898 in green underglaze; SPF
mark of hammer, sickle and cog, SUPREMATISM, 474, and
signature 'Suetin', all in black overglaze.
LPF inventory letters and the number, 2940.

154
Ilia G. Chashnik
Goblet with Suprematist design.
Marks:
None. The word 'SUPREMATISM', 474, a black square within a
square and the signature 'Il. Chashnik', all in Cyrillic in black
overglaze.
LPF inventory letters and the number, 3136.

153

154

155
Vasilii V. Kandinsky
Cup and saucer with green rims, early 1920s.
Cup Height 2 $\frac{11}{16}$ in. (6.8 cm.)
Saucer Dm. 5 $\frac{1}{2}$ in. (14 cm.)
156
Vasilii V. Kandinsky
Cup and saucer with pink rims, early 1920s.
Cup Height 2 in. (5 cm.)
Saucer Dm. 5 $\frac{3}{4}$ in. (14.5 cm.)

155

156

157

157

Coffee can and saucer based on a design by
Vasilii V. Kandinsky

Coffee can and saucer with black rims and coloured compositions, based on designs by Kandinsky, covering them.

Kandinsky's designs for porcelain, made in the early twenties, were used both by the State Porcelain Factory in Petrograd and the Dulevo Porcelain Factory near Moscow.

Marks:

Cup IPF monogram for Nicholas II, 1914 in green underglaze; SPF mark of hammer, sickle and cog, plus '1923' and pattern number 'No. 448/21', all in blue overglaze. Height $2\frac{1}{2}$ in. (6.2 cm.)

Saucer IPF monogram for Nicholas II, 1914 in green underglaze; SPF mark of hammer, sickle and cog, plus '1923' and pattern number 'No. 448', all in blue overglaze. Dm. $5\frac{11}{16}$ in. (14.5 cm.)

158

Vladimir V. Lebedev or **Ivan A. Puni (Jean Pougny)**

Teapot painted with a Suprematist design on the front and back of its body and on its lid, with Cyrillic letters in the design. They spell out, front, 'Revolution'; back, 'Communist'; and lid, 'Russia'.

Both Lebedev and Puni made designs for the SPF but they did not paint on porcelain. Their designs were executed by factory artists. Neither authorities on Soviet porcelain, nor those on twentieth-century Russian art, to whom photographs of the teapot or the teapot itself were shown, could make up their minds with absolute certainty about the artist.

Marks:

SPF mark of hammer, sickle and cog in green underglaze; the date, '1923' and pattern '567/3' in black overglaze.
Height 5 in. (13 cm.)

158

159
Nikolai F. Lapshin
Large plate with an abstract design in black and pink on a white background. Other examples from this service can be found in the Ludwig Collection, Cologne, and in the Badisches Landesmuseum, Karlsruhe. This service earned Lapshin a gold medal at the Exposition Internationale des Arts Décoratifs, Paris, 1925.
Marks:
IPF monogram obliterated by a diamond-shaped green blob; SPF mark of hammer, sickle and cog in blue overglaze. Though undated, this plate was decorated sometime between 1921 and 1923. Dm. $10\frac{3}{4}$ in. (27.3 cm.)

160
Vladimir V. Lebedev (attributed)
Small plate with a yellow border and a Cubist design of a landscape with house in the cavetto. A similar plate was exhibited at, and illustrated in the catalogue of the first Soviet exhibition held abroad, in Berlin, at the Galerie van Diemen in 1922.
Marks:
IPF monogram obliterated with an oval green blob; SPF mark of hammer, sickle and cog plus '1921' in blue overglaze.
Dm. $8\frac{1}{2}$ in. (21.5 cm.)

159

160

161
Kazimir S. Malevich
Half cup.
Marks:
None. Made at the SPF in 1923.
Height: 2 3/8 in. (6 cm.)
LPF inventory letters and number, 2117.

161

162
Kazimir S. Malevich
Suprematist teapot in an ordered scale of the forms of
cylinder and sphere to curve, and of square to rectangle.
Balancing the masses and thus achieving dynamic tension
was one of the objectives of Suprematism. Malevich did
not intend it to be a functional object but rather a study
of the interaction of forms.
Marks:
None. Made at the SPF in 1923.
Height: 6½ in. (16.5 cm.)
LPF inventory letters and the number, 2114.

162

163

Plate based on a design by **Kazimir S. Malevich**
Plate with colourful Suprematist design. In 1920, in Vitebsk, Malevich wrote the text and made the lithos for *Suprematism: 34 Drawings* (published in 1921). This album provided a survey and graphic paraphrase of the major Suprematist paintings of 1915 onwards. The design on this plate, with slight variations, is the same as the lithograph in the album entitled 'In Suprematist space'.
Marks:
SPF mark of hammer, sickle and cog, '1923', 'No. 660/21' and 'Po riz Malevicha' (based on drawing by Malevich), all in black overglaze. Also, the word 'SUPREMATISM' in Cyrillic and a black square within a square, the LPF inventory letters and a number, 2125. The black square held special meaning for Malevich, and became a symbol of the followers of Unovis and of Suprematism. Dm. $9\frac{3}{4}$ in. (24.8 cm.)

164

Kazimir S. Malevich
Plate with Suprematist design. The design is the same as that of the lithograph in *Suprematism: 34 Drawings* entitled 'Aeroplane Flying'. The oil painting of 'Aeroplane Flying' (1915), is in the collection of the Museum of Modern Art, New York.
Marks:
IPF monogram for Nicholas II, 1898 in green underglaze; SPF mark of hammer, sickle and cog, plus '1923' and 'N. 660/7' in blue overglaze; also, in Cyrillic, 'Po riz Malevicha' (based on drawing by Malevich) in blue overglaze. Dm. $9\frac{3}{4}$ in. (24.8 cm.)

165

Nikolai M. Suetin
Suprematist inkstand. This is designed as a horizontal *architekton*. In 1915 Malevich had begun experimenting with three-dimensional idealized architectural drawings. He called these 'Planity'. At the State Institute of Painterly Culture, Leningrad (Inkhuk), during the 1920s, assisted by Suetin and Chashnik, he concentrated on these architectural projects, and also made the three-dimensional models in plaster and wood known as *architektony*.
Marks
Incised initials 'I.K.', probably those of the factory artist Ivan Kuznetsov.
Height: 5 in. (12.5 cm.)
Depth and width: $5\frac{3}{4}$ in. (14.5 cm.)

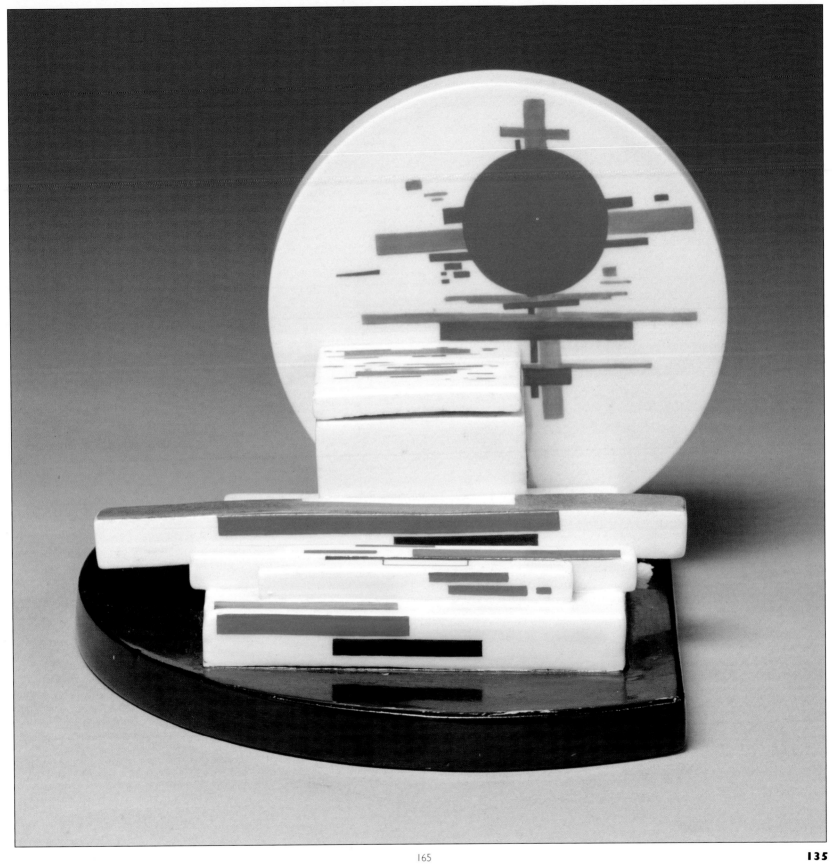

166

167

168

166/167/168
Nikolai M. Suetin
Three plates with Suprematist designs in red.
Marks
Identical on all three plates. SPF mark of hammer, sickle and cog
plus SUPREMATISM, 474, a black square within a square, and
signed 'Suetin', all in Cyrillic and in black overglaze.
Plate a/ LPF inventory letters and number 2936;
Plate b/ LPF inventory letters and number 2934;
Plate c/ LPF inventory letters and number 2937.
169
Nikolai M. Suetin
Plate with Suprematist design in black.

169

170

Cup and saucer based on a design by **Nikolai M. Suetin**
Coffee cup and saucer decorated with a Suprematist design.
Marks:
Cup IPF monogram for Nicholas II, 1896 in green underglaze;
SPF mark of hammer, sickle and cog plus '1923' in blue
overglaze. Pattern number '474/002' in iron-red overglaze.
Height 2½ in. (6.2 cm.)
Saucer IPF monogram for Nicholas II, 1914 in green
underglaze; SPF mark of hammer, sickle and cog, '1923', in blue
overglaze. Pattern number '474' in iron-red overglaze.
Dm. 5¹¹⁄₁₆ in. (14.5 cm.)

171
Nikolai M. Suetin
Suprematist coffee service, 1923.
Marks:
Cup SPF mark of hammer, sickle and cog, the date, 1923, also
'SUPREMATISM, 474/9' and Suetin's signature, both printed and
written, the first, 'N. Suetin', the second' 'Suetin', all in Cyrillic in
black overglaze.
LPF inventory letters and the number, 2967.
It is rare to see the date 1923 used in conjunction with the
number 474 and the word 'SUPREMATISM' – the latter two
are usually sufficient indication that a piece may be dated to that
year.

171

172
Nikolai M. Suetin
Two rectangular ceramic vases. Prototypes created in 1933.
Suetin used this form, and variations on it, time and again in
ceramics and in architecture.
Marks:
None.
I Height 9¾ in. (24.7 cm.) Dm. 3¾ in. (9.5 cm.)
II Height 3⅞ in. (9.8 cm.) Dm. 3¾ in. (9.5 cm.)

173

Nikolai M. Suetin

Suprematist tea service consisting of eight pieces, made in 1932, the year Suetin became artistic director of the Lomonosov Porcelain Factory. By this time most artists elsewhere in the Soviet Union, were turning to Socialist Realism.

The layout shown above was painted, in the form of a chart, onto the back of the tray, in black, by Suetin. It specifies how the service should be laid out when not in use. This indicates that although Suetin considered each separate piece to be a Suprematist work, he also considered the arrangement and interaction of the whole to be important. The service has been arranged as shown on Suetin's chart.

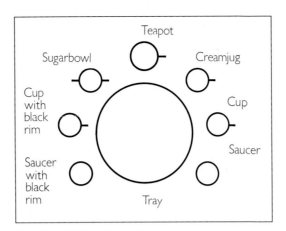

Teapot

Sugarbowl   Creamjug

Cup
with
black   Cup
rim

Saucer

Saucer
with
black
rim   Tray

173

Chronology

1905 Civil unrest throughout Russia culminates in the so-called First Russian Revolution and the establishment of a national legislative assembly, the Duma, with limited powers. Most dissenters were either exiled to Siberia or had fled abroad.

1908 In May, Diaghilev takes the Russian opera to Paris. Chaliapin sings the title role in *Boris Godunov*.

1909 Diaghilev's first Ballets Russes season in Paris.

1913 The Romanov dynasty celebrates its 300th anniversary. The celebrations include a general pardon for many exiled Russian political figures.

1914 In June, Archduke Francis Ferdinand is assassinated at Sarajevo. Austria declares war on Serbia. In August Germany declares war on Russia. St. Petersburg is renamed Petrograd.

1915 Collapse of Russia's southern front before an Austro-German offensive. In December, Rasputin is assassinated.

1916 Heavy Russian losses demoralize the army.

1917 22 February – 3 March (old style) the Revolution begins. The Duma meets, forming a Provisional Government headed by Prince Lvov, with the agreement of the Petrograd Soviet. Nicholas II abdicates in favour of his brother, Grand Duke Michael, who abdicates twenty-four hours later, ending the Romanov dynasty. During April and May, Lenin, Trotsky, Lunacharsky and other leading Bolsheviks return to Russia. In June, the First All-Russian Congress of Soviets meets in Petrograd. In July, a coalition government is formed under Kerensky. The Second All-Russian Congress of Soviets in Petrograd in October grants total power to the Soviet. The October Revolution establishes the new Soviet regime. In November, Lunacharsky is appointed Commissar for Narkompros, the Commissariat for Enlightenment, and immediately starts to organize the cultural and educational life of post-revolutionary Russia. In December, an armistice is concluded with Imperial Germany and peace negotiations open at Brest-Litovsk.

1918 In January, IZO, a special visual arts section, is established within Narkompros. Many artists and critics of the avant-garde take administrative, teaching, research or consultative jobs with the various branches of IZO.
In February, the first Soviet Constitution is adopted by the Fifth All-Russian Congress of Soviets.
In March, the Treaty of Brest-Litovsk is finally signed, and the capital is moved from Petrograd to Moscow.
In April, the Academy of Arts in Petrograd, as well as the old art schools in Moscow and various provincial cities, are replaced by the Svomas (Free State Art Schools).
In July, the Imperial family is assassinated.

1919 Civil war on several fronts throughout the year. In March, the Third International (Comintern) is formed and the First World Congress of Comintern meets in Moscow.

1920 In May, Inkhuk (Institute of Painterly Culture) is organized in Moscow with affiliations in Petrograd, Vitebsk and elsewhere. In September, the Svomas are replaced in their turn by the VKhUTEMAS (Higher State Technical Art Studios).
The Congress of the Peoples of the East is held at Baku under the chairmanship of Zinoviev.
A disastrous harvest is followed by famine and a general collapse of the economy.

1921 In March, there is a naval mutiny at Kronstadt – both officers and sailors are disillusioned by the Bolshevik commissarocracy. The New Economic Policy comes into effect, partially restoring a free enterprise system in order to encourage production.

1922 In December the Union of Soviet Socialist Republics (U.S.S.R.) is established.

1924 Lenin dies on 21 January. On the 26th, Petrograd is renamed Leningrad. Stalin and Trotsky compete for power.

1926 In April the U.S.S.R. and Germany sign a treaty of friendship and neutrality. In September VKhUTEMAS is replaced with VKhUTEIN (Higher State Art-Technical Institute).

1927 In November Stalin expels Trotsky from the Party.

1928 The first Five-Year Plan is inaugurated.

Artists' biographies

Adamovich
Mikhail Mikhailovich
1884–1947
Graduated from the Stroganov School of Art and Industrial Design, Moscow (1907); sent to Italy on a scholarship to study decorative art (1907–09); upon returning worked on decorative paintings for the interiors of buildings in Moscow and St. Petersburg (1909–13); invited to Greece and commissioned by the Greek government to produce a mosaic for the tomb of King George I; military service (1914–17). He worked in the arts department of the State Porcelain Factory in the building of the old Baron A. Stieglitz School (1918–19); served in the Red Army (1919–21); returned to the State Porcelain Factory (1921–3). His Red Army years made a deep impression on Adamovich and inspired a series of plates. Worked at the Volkhov Factory near Novgorod (1924–7); painter at Dulevo Factory (?1927–33). Adamovich then returned to the decorative painting of public buildings in Moscow (1934–47). He took part in several exhibitions organized by various societies: the World of Art (1922, 1924), the Artists' Commune (1922), and the Association of Artists of Revolutionary Russia (1924), and also participated in the *Exposition Internationale des Arts Décoratifs* in Paris at which he was awarded a medal (1925).

Altman
Natan Isaevich
1889–1970
Painter, graphic artist and theatre designer. Studied at art school in Odessa (1902–07) and at the Free Russian Academy of Marie Vasilieva, Paris (1910–12). From 1910 onwards contributed to many avant-garde exhibitions including those known as the 'Knave of Diamonds' and '0.10' (at which Malevich launched Suprematism). Taught at Svomas (Free Art Studios) in Petrograd (1918–20). Member of IZO Narkompros (Visual Arts Section of the Commissariat of Enlightenment). Sketched portraits of Lenin from life; decorated Uritsky Square (Palace Square), Petrograd, for the first anniversary of the October Revolution (1918), later using one of the details of this decoration as the central motif for a propaganda plate. Lived and worked in Paris (1929–35). Returned to Leningrad in 1936. From the 1920s, in addition to painting he worked a great deal as a theatrical designer and book illustrator.

Briantseva
Maria Alexandrovna
1885–1942
Graduated from the School for the Deaf and Dumb, St. Petersburg (1904); studied at the Baron A. Stieglitz School of Technical Design, where she worked at painting on porcelain, leather embossing, architectural drawings and sculpture (1904–13); in 1913 started work at the Imperial Porcelain Factory and continued working there as a painter-copyist after the October Revolution until 1941 – the rest of her working life. Although Briantseva did not create original designs, she was a superbly trained artist, highly skilled at painting the figurines of Natalya Danko, and executing the designs of other artists.

Brusketti-Mitrokhina
Alisa Yakovlevna
1872–1942
Graduated from the Moscow School of Painting, Sculpture and Architecture (1901); worked as a sculptor at the Abramtsevo Ceramic Studio, Moscow, until 1905; taught design at the Commercial School in Tver (1905–09); worked at the ceramic workshop of the Society for the Encouragement of the Arts, St. Petersburg (1909–14); taught the art of ornament in the Arts and Industry School in Pskov (1915–19); worked on a series of genre statuettes of 'city types' in Petrograd for the State Porcelain Factory (1918–20) and also on small figurines of ballerinas and athletes (1930). Took part in exhibitions from 1908, among them those organized by the Brotherhood of Wanderers and the Artists' Commune (1921–2).

Chashnik
Ilia Grigorevich
1902–29
Apprenticed to an optico-mechanical workshop in Vitebsk, and simultaneously studied art in the studio of Yurii Pen (1917–19); attended VKhUTEMAS in Moscow (1920); graduated from the Vitebsk Popular Art Institute, where he studied under first Chagall, then Malevich (1922); participated in organization of POSNOVIS (Followers of the New Art) which was later renamed UNOVIS (Affirmers of the New Art). Participated in all exhibitions of the UNOVIS group. In 1922 he followed Malevich to Petrograd. Between 1923 and 1924 worked at the State Porcelain Factory with Suetin; from 1924 worked at the State Institute of Artistic Culture (GINKhUK) as assistant to Malevich in his work on architectural models; from 1925 to 1926 worked with Suetin and the architect Alexander Nikolsky.

Chekhonin (Tchekhonine)
Sergei Vasilievich
1878–1936
Studied at the drawing school of the Society for the Encouragement of the Arts (1896–7); took lessons in painting from Ilya Repin at Princess Maria Tenisheva's private art school in St. Petersburg (1897–1900); worked at sculpture and ceramics in the Abramtsevo Ceramic Studio in Moscow (1904–06); contributed caricatures and cartoons to revolutionary journals (1905–06); visited Paris (1906); working at the ceramics factory of Pyotr Vaulin at Kikerino near St. Petersburg, made a number of majolica panels for buildings in St. Petersburg (1907); worked on illustrations for many magazines and books, considered the most outstanding book illustrator in pre-revolutionary Russia; received first prize for new typography design from Leman publishers (1912). In 1910 joined the revived World of Art society and contributed regularly to its exhibitions until

1924; was a specialist consultant on artistic crafts to the Ministry of Agriculture and directed a school for decorative work with and on enamel at Rostov-Yaroslavky (1913–18); head of the art section of the State Porcelain Factory over two periods, 1918–23 and 1925–7 (for which he organized a temporary art and design section at the former Baron A. Stieglitz School); artistic director of the Volkhov Factory near Novgorod (1923–4); Chekhonin painted many memorable plates, cups and saucers himself and created hundreds of compositions, drawings, monograms and anniversary marks for the factory; he also attracted a number of outstanding painters and graphic designers to the factory; represented at the *Exposition Internationale des Arts Décoratifs* in Paris (1925, gold medal); emigrated to Paris in 1928; worked as a designer for Nikita Baliev's 'Chauve-souris' cabaret and for the Ballets Russes Vera Nemtchinova in Paris (1929); worked for *Vogue* magazine; designed porcelain, jewellery and posters.

Danko
Elena Y.
1898–1942
Studied at the drawing school of Alexander Murashko in Kiev (1915) and in Moscow at the studios of Ilya Mashkov and Fedor Rerberg (1915–18). Between 1918 and 1941 she worked off and on as a painter at the State Porcelain Factory, mainly decorating the works of her sister Natalya, and some special services. Wrote plays for Shaporina-Yakovleva's puppet theatre (1919–20); studied the history of ceramics (1922); was a member of the literary board of the 'Theatre of the Young Spectator' in Petrograd and collaborated in the production of three plays (1923). In 1925 Danko became secretary of the Leningrad poets' organization. She was a well-known author of children's books and wrote a history of the Lomonosov Porcelain Factory.

Danko
Natalya Y.
1892–1942
Sculptor. Studied at Stroganov School of Art and Industrial Design, Moscow (1900–02); the State Art School, Vilnius, and the studio of Yalmar Yanson (1906–08); the workshop of Maria Dillon and the studio of the sculptor Leonid Sherwood, St. Petersburg (1908–09). From 1909 worked in the workshop of the sculptor Vasilii Kuznetsov. Participated in the execution of reliefs and sculptures for buildings in Moscow, St. Petersburg and Kiev, and for the Russian pavilions at exhibitions in Turin and Rome (1910–11). From 1914 worked as Kuznetsov's assistant at Imperial Porcelain Factory. From 1919 to 1941 Danko headed the sculpture workshop at the renamed State Porcelain Factory. She created 311 different items, including hundreds of figurines of contemporary genre characters, portraits and satirical statuettes. She also worked on exquisite pipes, brooches and scent bottles. In the 1930s she made decorative sculptures and bas-reliefs for the Sverdlov Square and the River Station (Khimki) buildings of the metro in Moscow.

143

Danko's work was shown at the *Exposition Internationale des Arts Décoratifs*, Paris (1925); the International Exhibition of Art in Industry and Decorative Arts, Monza (1927), and the World Exhibition, Paris (1937), and was awarded gold medals at all three. She had one-woman shows in Leningrad in 1929 and 1946.

Freze

Varvara Petrovna
1883–1970
Studied at the drawing school of the Society for the Encouragement of the Arts, St. Petersburg (1900–04) and at the Baron A. Stieglitz Central School of Technical Design, specializing in painting porcelain (1904–10). She worked at the State Porcelain Factory as an artist-painter over a number of periods – 1918–19, 1921–4, 1926–8 and 1934–9. From 1924 to 1926 she painted porcelain for factories of the Novgorod Porcelain Trust. She probably went there at the instigation of Chekhonin who himself spent two years at the Volkhov Factory and whose designs Freze frequently executed. Illustrated scientific publications (1939–41); camouflaged buildings in Leningrad (1941–2); was an arts teacher (1945–50); then became a lecturer at the Faculty of Artistic Ceramics at the Vera I. Mukhina (formerly Stieglitz) Central School of Industrial Design, Leningrad.

Gaush

Liubov Nikolaevna
1877–1943
Graduated from the drawing school of the Society for the Encouragement of the Arts, St. Petersburg (1909); attended the academy of Rodolphe Julian, Paris. She took part in several exhibitions from 1909, among them the 'World of Art' and that of the Association of K. Kostandi. She painted still lifes, landscapes, portraits and miniatures on bone and also embroidered. Worked at the State Porcelain Factory (1919–22) where she executed a series of plates with portraits of the Decembrists, plates with views of Petrograd and of Rome, and flower patterns.

Girshfeld

Natalya A.
Dates unknown
Worked at the State Porcelain Factory from 1919 until 1922, when she was made redundant.

Golenkina

Alisa Rudolfovna
1884–1970
Graduated from the Baron A. Stieglitz School of Technical Design, St. Petersburg (1910), where she had specialized in artistic work on leather; worked as painter and designer at the State Porcelain Factory (1919–24); she created many compositions and sketches, mainly of agitprop and allegorical subjects and portraits; in later years worked at the All-Russia Institute of Botany as an illustrator.

Ivashintsova

Maria Ivanovna
1882–1957
Studied in the Higher Art School, St. Petersburg Academy of Arts (1908–15). Worked in Petrograd and Moscow as an illustrator of books and magazines including *New Satyricon* (1915–17). Worked at the State Porcelain Factory (1918–20). Both her graphic work and her work on porcelain were shown in many exhibitions including those of the Fellowship of Wanderers and the Association of Artists of Revolutionary Russia (1923, 1924), the exhibition of artistic products of the State Workshop of IZO Narkompros in Moscow, and the exhibition of products from the State Porcelain Factory in Petrograd (both 1919).

Kandinsky

Vasilii Vasilievich
1866–1944
Studied at the Faculty of Law of Moscow University (1886–92); in 1893 was appointed to the Department of Law at Moscow University. In 1896 he decided to dedicate himself to art; went to Munich where he studied at the Anton Azbé School and met Alexei Jawlensky (1897–9); in 1900 studied at the Royal Academy, Munich. Between 1902 and 1914 lived in Munich but made frequent trips to Russia; he was a founder member of The Phalanx (1901), the New Munich Society of the Arts (1909), *Der Blaue Reiter* (1911) and from 1910 was a member of the 'Knave of Diamonds' group and participated in the 'Donkey's Tail' exhibition; was Munich correspondent for the St. Petersburg magazine *Apollon*; from 1914 to 1921 lived in Moscow (except for the period between December 1915 and March 1916, which he spent in Stockholm); from 1918 onwards was one of the chief organizers of artistic life in Russia. In 1918 became a member of the collegium of IZO Narkompros and the author of a plan for a network of contemporary art museums. From 1919 to 1921 he was a professor at the State Free Arts Workshops in Petrograd and in 1920 he became a professor at Moscow University and a member of the Institute of Artistic Culture (INKhUK); in 1921 he was vice-president of the Russian Academy of Artistic Sciences. At the end of 1921 he went to Weimar to teach at the Bauhaus. In 1933 he moved to France. He was active as a painter and writer until his death. In 1921 he made several designs to be used on porcelain.

Kobyletskaya

Zinaida Viktorovna
1880–1957
Studied painting porcelain at the drawing school of the Society for the Encouragement of the Arts, St. Petersburg (graduated 1910), and at factories in Denmark, Sweden and France (1910–12). Worked at the Imperial Porcelain Factory (1912–14) and the State Porcelain Factory (1918–23). Painted a number of agitational plates. In 1924 she made drawings for the Volkhov Factory, Novgorod, and returned to the Lomonosov Porcelain Factory (1926–1932) where she produced 1500 sketches and drawings for the factory.

From 1932 onwards Kobyletskaya illustrated scientific works, chiefly the botanical publications of the Academy of Sciences of the Soviet Union, including 'Flora of the USSR' and 'Flora of Tadjikistan'. Her work was shown in all the exhibitions that took place abroad and in the Soviet Union in the 1920s and '30s, including the *Exposition Internationale des Arts Décoratifs*, Paris, where she was awarded the Diploma of Honour (1925), the International Exhibition of Arts in Industry and Decorative Arts in Monza, where she was awarded a gold medal (1927) and in the World Exhibitions in Paris and New York (1937 and 1939).

Kustodiev

Boris Mikhailovich
1878–1927
Painter, portrait painter, theatrical designer and sculptor. Studied at the Academy of Arts, St. Petersburg (1896–1903); was sent to France and Spain on a grant from the Academy (1904); illustrated satirical magazines (1905); participated in Union of Russian Artists (1907–10); became member of the World of Art in 1910; in 1923 was commissioned by the State Porcelain Factory to make two figurines: 'The Accordionist' and 'Girl Dancing'. These two figures were reproduced repeatedly over many years at the State Porcelain Factory. Kustodiev sculpted many other figurines representing characters in his paintings, such as 'Merchant's Wife with Cat' and 'Merchant in a Fur Coat', but they were not reproduced by the factory. Travelled in Italy, France, Germany and Switzerland (1911 and 1913); took part in many exhibitions. One-man exhibitions were held in Petrograd/Leningrad (1920 and 1928) and Moscow (1929, 1947, 1952, 1968).

Kuznetsov

Vasilii Vasilievich
1881–1923
Sculptor. Studied sculpture at the Academy of Arts, St. Petersburg (1901–08); worked on decorative reliefs for buildings (banks, schools and private houses) in Kiev and St. Petersburg (1908–14); designed friezes and figures for the Russian pavilions at the International Exhibitions in Rome (1910) and Turin (1911). From 1914 to 1917 headed the sculpture workshop of the Imperial Porcelain Factory, and stayed on in the same position after the October Revolution, until 1919 at the State Porcelain Factory. He received a state commission to model a bust of Karl Marx in porcelain in 1918. In the same year he created 'The Red Guard', the first porcelain figurine representing a man of the Soviet era. In 1919, due to the difficult food situation in Petrograd, he returned home to the District of Saratov, from where he continued to send his models and designs to the factory.

Lapshin

Nikolai Feodorovich
1889–1942
Graphic artist and painter. Studied at the drawing school of the Society for the Encouragement of the Arts,

St. Petersburg, and at the studio of Yan Tsionglinsky and Mikhail Bernstein. From 1922 participated in exhibitions including 'New Tendencies in Art', 'Petrograd Artists of all Tendencies' and 'Four Arts'. Painted and designed for porcelain at the State Porcelain Factory (1920–23). Exhibited abroad, Leipzig (1927), Cologne (1928), Winterthur (1929) and Paris (1931). Lived and worked in Leningrad.

Lebedev
Vladimir Vasilievich
1891–1967
Graphic artist and painter. Studied drawing at the studio of Alexander Titov, St. Petersburg (1909); workshop of Franz Rubo (1909–11); Academy of Arts (1912–16) and simultaneously studied at the School of Painting, Drawing and Sculpture of Mikhail Bernstein and Leonid Sherwood. From 1912 participated in many exhibitions. Worked as an illustrator of magazines (1911–17). Designed for porcelain decoration and the State Porcelain Factory produced a series of articles bearing his designs (1918–19). He taught in the Petrograd State Free Art Studios (1918–21). Designed propaganda posters for the ROSTA windows with Mayakovsky (1920–21). In 1928 he held a one-man exhibition in Leningrad. Worked on posters for TASS windows (1942–5).

Lebedeva
Maria Vasilievna
1895–1942
Graduated from the drawing school of the Society for the Encouragement of the Arts in St. Petersburg (1917). Studied with Ivan Bilibin. While at the school she was twice sent on tour, once abroad and once across Russia. She toured the northern Russian towns with her school friend Alexandra Shchekotikhina-Pototskaya who later married Bilibin. After school, she worked as a graphic designer on books and posters, and as a decorative artist on ceilings and murals. She started work at the State Porcelain Factory in 1919 in the department of painting, then located at the Stieglitz School. Between 1919 and 1923, and 1934 and 1940 she produced many interesting designs for porcelain. From 1924 to 1927 she taught applied art in the Arts Technical School of Vitebsk and from 1933 to 1936 in the Minsk Art Institute. She took part in many exhibitions including those of the World of Art and Society of Painters; the *Exposition Internationale des Arts Décoratifs* in Paris (1925) and the exhibitions of Russian art in Vienna and Berlin (1930).

Malevich
Kazimir Severinovich
1878–1935
Studied at drawing school, Kiev (1895–6), and at Moscow School of Painting, Sculpture and Architecture (1904–05); worked at studio of Fedor Rerberg, Moscow (1905–10); from 1910 participated in exhibitions including 'Knave of Diamonds', 'Donkey's Tail', 'Union of Youth', 'Tramway V' and '0.10' (1915) – the latter the first showing of

Suprematist paintings; designed sets and costumes for opera 'Victory over the Sun' (libretto by Kruchenykh and music by Matiushin, 1913); published pamphlet 'From Cubism to Suprematism' (1915); active on various levels within the Visual Arts Section of the People's Commissariat for Enlightenment (1918). Between 1919 and 1922 worked at Vitebsk Popular Art Institute; co-organized UNOVIS (Affirmers of New Art) which attracted many young artists including Chashnik, Ermolaeva, El Lissitzky and Suetin. In 1922 moved to Petrograd where he worked for the Leningrad branch of the Institute of Artistic Culture; from 1923 until the late '20s; active on various levels: worked on designs for ceramics; his teapot and 'half cups' produced at the State Porcelain Factory (1923); wrote many essays on art; experimented with the architectural possibilities of Suprematism, inventing the concepts of 'arkhitektony', 'planity' and 'zemlianity' (1927); visited Warsaw and Berlin with a one-man exhibition; established contact with the Bauhaus; returned to figurative painting in about 1930.

Matveev
Alexander Terentevich
1878–1960
Studied at the drawing school of A. P. Bogolyubov in Saratov (1896–9); and at Moscow School of Painting, Sculpture and Architecture (1899–1902); worked at Abramtsevo Ceramic Studio in Moscow (1901–05); visited Paris 1906–07; sculptor, ceramics factory of Pyotr Vaulin at Kikerino near St. Petersburg (1907–12); he was a member of a number of artistic groups and took part in the exhibitions of the World of Art, Blue Rose, Golden Fleece and Knave of Diamonds groups and the Society of Russian Sculptors. Visited Florence, Rome and Naples (1913). His work was shown in many exhibitions abroad including 'The First Russian Exhibition' in Berlin (1922) and the *Exposition Internationale des Arts Décoratifs*, Paris, where he was awarded a gold medal (1925). From 1918 he taught in the State Free Art Workshops in Petrograd and the Institute of Painting, Sculpture and Architecture of the Academy of Arts. He was Dean of the Sculpture Faculty, and later became Director (1932–5). Between 1919 and 1921 he modelled ten small powerful figures of nude women. Four of them were produced in limited numbers from 1923 onwards by the State Porcelain Factory. They are known as 'Standing Woman With Cup', 'Woman Putting on Slipper', 'Seated Woman With Bowl', 'Woman Putting on Stocking'. In 1926 he made two genre figures, 'The Carpenter' and 'The Market Gardener' which were also produced as porcelain figurines at the factory.

Mosyagin
Vladimir Sergeevich
d. 1923
In 1922 some of his sketches were used by the State Porcelain Factory on plates intended for export. He participated in exhibitions at the House of Arts (1921) and the Artists' Commune (1922) in Petrograd.

Narbut
Georgi Ivanovich
1886–1920
Well-known Ukrainian graphic designer and illustrator. Attended University of St. Petersburg where he read history and philology (1906); studied in the studio of Elizaveta Zvantseva, St. Petersburg (1907–08), and at the Holloszy Art School in Munich (1909). Participated in the exhibitions of the Union of Russian Artists, the New Society and the World of Art. In 1918 he returned to the Ukraine and was a professor at the Academy of Arts in Kiev. He never worked at the State Porcelain Factory but after his death, at the suggestion of Chekhonin, his silhouette designs were used on a series of objects produced by the factory specifically for export (1920–23).

Radonich
Bazilka Stepanovna
b.1884
Born in Montenegro, in 1905 she moved to Russia. Popular rumour said she was the sister of the Queen of Montenegro. From 1920 to 1924 she worked as a painter and designer at the State Porcelain Factory. In 1924 she moved to Italy. Radonich died in an old people's home in Milan in the late 1970s.

Rozendorf
Yelizaveta Berngardovna
b. 1898
Worked at the State Porcelain Factory as a painter (1919–20). She created a large number of interesting agit-designs. From the early 1920s she lived in Estonia. In 1923 she took part in an exhibition of decorative art in Tallinn; between 1923 and 1927 she participated in exhibitions organized by the Central Society of Estonian Artists as a graphic artist and painter.

Shchekotikhina-Pototskaya
Alexandra Vasilievna
1892–1967
Born in the Ukraine into a family of Old Believers. Studied in the drawing school of the Society for the Encouragement of the Arts, St. Petersburg, under Nikolai Roerich and Ivan Bilibin (1908–15); in 1910 the school sent her on a tour of northern Russia with her schoolmate, Maria Lebedeva; in 1913 she was sent to Greece, Italy and France. While in Paris she studied at the Académie Ranson, in the studios of Maurice Denis, François Vallotton and Paul Serusier. Between 1912 and 1920 she designed for the theatre, including costume sketches for 'Snegourotchka' (The Snow Maiden) in 1912, for Roerich and Stravinsky's ballet, 'The Rite of Spring', for Diaghilev's 1913 production, and for Borodin's opera 'Prince Igor', for Diaghilev's 1914 London production. (Roerich was the chief designer for both Diaghilev productions; Shchekotikhina worked under him.) From 1915 participated in the exhibitions of the World of Art. She worked as a painter and designer at the State Porcelain Factory creating many designs for porcelain and

models for sculpture between 1918 and 1923, and 1936 and 1953; in 1923 she went abroad and travelled with her second husband, Ivan Bilibin, in Egypt, Ethiopia, Syria and Palestine, studying and sketching monuments, national costumes and regional crafts. From 1925 to 1936 she, Bilibin and her son by her first husband lived at 23, Boulevard Pasteur in Paris. While travelling in the Middle East and living in Paris she made a number of sketches for the Lomonosov Porcelain Factory. In Paris, she decorated white Sèvres and Limoges porcelain, and worked as an illustrator and theatrical designer. She had a one-woman show at the Galérie Druet (1926) and took part in the exhibitions at the Salon d'Automne and the Salon des Indépendants. In 1936 she returned to Leningrad with Bilibin and her son and resumed work at the Lomonosov Porcelain Factory under the direction of Suetin. In 1937, together with Bilibin, she made sketches for the costumes and sets of the Rimsky-Korsakov opera 'The Tale of Tsar Saltan' for the State Theatre of Opera and Ballet. Held a one-woman show in Leningrad in 1955.

Sherbakov
Valentin Semyonovich
1880–1957
Studied at the Kazan Art School (1894–1900); attended the Academy of Arts in St. Petersburg (1900–09), simultaneously studied ancient Russian painting in the Archeological Institute; in 1907 made a journey to the old Russian towns of Kostroma, Yaroslav and Rostov Yaroslavsky to study and sketch frescoes and seventeenth-century monuments. In 1913 visited the Balkans and Serbia, again to study and sketch frescoes and twelfth- and thirteenth-century architectural monuments; his architectural sketches and copies of frescoes were exhibited in St. Petersburg. In 1915 he visited northern Russia and the provinces of Novgorod and Pskov; in 1917 started work in the art section of the State Porcelain Factory and produced one hundred compositions for the factory within a year; worked for factory until 1922, simultaneously working in Kazan as a theatre designer; in 1922 opened an enamel workshop in Petrograd at the Academy of Arts. Between 1928 and 1931 taught in the State Art and Industry Technical School of VKhUTEIN in Leningrad, then between 1949 and 1954 was professor at the Vera Mukhina (former Stieglitz) School of Industrial Design, Leningrad.

Suetin
Nikolai Mikhailovich
1897–1954
One of the leading Suprematist artists. Painter, graphic artist, designer and ceramics painter. Served in the army in Vitebsk (1915–17); studied in the Vitebsk Popular Art Institute under Malevich (1918–22); was a member of the UNOVIS group. After 1922 lived in Leningrad. In 1923 he started work at the State Porcelain Factory, creating new forms for ceramics and painting porcelain with Suprematist designs. He was a member of the Institute of Art Culture (INKhUK), 1923–26. Worked at experimental laboratory of

the Institute of Art History, Leningrad (1927–30). He was chief artist of the State Porcelain Factory between 1932 and 1954 and the chief artist and designer of the architectural and decorative aspects of the interiors of the Soviet pavilions for the World Fairs in Paris (1937) and New York (1939).

Tatevosyan
Oganes Karapetovish
1889–1974
Attended art classes at the Caucasus Society for the Encouragement of Fine Arts in Tiflis (1906); studied at the Moscow School of Painting, Sculpture and Architecture under Konstantin Korovine (1910–17); attended VKhUTEMAS in Moscow (1921–7). From 1917 he lived in Tashkent and was one of the organizers of the Samarkand Commune School (1918) and of other schools of painting and sculpture in Yerevan (1921). He was at the head of a group of ceramicists of VKhUTEMAS who prepared a series of sculptures and plates at the Dulevo Porcelain Factory near Moscow for the opening of the Sixth Congress of the Communist International (1921).

Timorev
Vasilii Porfirevich
1870–1942
Painter, graphic designer. Studied at the drawing school of the Association for the Encouragement of the Arts in St. Petersburg. Between 1890 and 1892 studied at the Higher Arts School of the Academy of Arts in St. Petersburg and in the workshop of Ilya Repin; studied etching in Paris, at the workshop of E. Kruglikova. While in Paris, also studied enamelling. Worked as graphic artist for the publisher Knebel in St. Petersburg between 1918 and 1921, and from 1922 worked mainly at book design. Towards the end of the 1920s worked at the State Porcelain Factory as a painter.

Trupiansky
Yakov Abramovich
1878–1955
Sculptor. Studied at Odessa Art School (1892–8); attended St. Petersburg Academy of Arts (1901–09); from 1910 to 1949 worked mainly at decorative sculpture and is responsible for many façades and interiors of buildings in Leningrad, Kharkov, Kiev and Odessa. Between 1921 and 1934 manager of artistic bronze section at the foundry works in Leningrad; from 1949 to 1955 taught design, painting and sculpture in the Leningrad Institute of Engineering Construction. The State Porcelain Factory produced two figurines from his models, a bust of Dostoevsky in 1922 and Chaliapin in the role of Boris Godunov in 1923.

Vesnin
Alexander Alexandrovich
1883–1959
Alexander was the youngest of the three Vesnin brothers

(the others were Leonid and Viktor) who worked closely together on many architectural and design projects from the 1910s to the early 1930s. Between 1901 and 1904, and 1911 and 1912 attended and eventually graduated from the Institute of Civil Engineering, St. Petersburg; during these years also studied painting with Konstantin Yuon in Moscow and Yan Tsionglinsky in St. Petersburg, and worked with his brother Viktor as an assistant for various architectural firms. Worked in Vladimir Tatlin's studio in Moscow, establishing close contact with Liubov Popova (1912–14); worked on agit-decorations for the streets and squares of Petrograd and Moscow (1918); designed sets for several stage productions; member of INKhUK (Institute of Artistic Culture), Moscow; keen supporter of Constructivism. From 1921 taught at the Moscow VKhUTEMAS, where together with Popova he taught colour construction. Participated in the '5 × 5 = 25' exhibition. Worked with his brothers on large architectural projects such as the Lenin Library and the Palace of Soviets, Moscow, and schemes for workers' cities.

Vilde
Rudolf Feodorovich
1868–?1942
Studied in the workshop of the Prokhovorov (now Trekhorny) Factory in Moscow. In 1895 entered the Baron A. Stieglitz Central School of Technical Design in St. Petersburg. Graduated 1899 with the qualification and title of 'expert graphic artist'. The school sent him to Germany, France and Italy on a scholarship (1899–1902). Upon returning to Russia he worked at interior decoration, copied decorative art designs for publications and took part in competitions and exhibitions, including the yearly competition of the Imperial Porcelain Factory. In 1905 he was chosen by the Imperial Porcelain Factory to become a graphic artist and modeller and from 1906 until the mid-1930s he was head of the painting workshop there. Between 1918 and 1923 he designed many agitprop plates with slogans. From 1938 he was head of the art section of the Volkhov Factory near Novgorod. His work received a gold medal at the *Exposition Internationale des Arts Décoratifs* in Paris (1925).

Vorobyevsky
Alexei Viktorovich
b.1906
Graduated from Art School in Pavlosk near Leningrad (1926). Since that time has worked at the Lomonosov Porcelain Factory in Leningrad. He is a master of decorative painting and ornamental composition on porcelain. He was named People's Artist of the RSFSR (1981).

Vyechegzhanin
Georgi Vladimirovich
1906–50
Son of the graphic artist Vladimir Levitsky and Lydia Vyechegzhanina, he took his mother's name and was adopted by Chekhonin, her second husband. Made some

sketches for the State Porcelain Factory (1919–20); studied at the Academy of Art, Leningrad (1924–9); worked as a graphic designer (1932–42); during the war worked as an artist for the Red Army; between 1945 and 1950 painter-architect at the Leningrad Department of Arts Foundation. (See caption for plate no. 60.)

Vyechegzhanin
Pyotr Vladimirovich (Pierre Ino)
b.1904
Son of the graphic artist Vladimir Levitsky and Lydia Vyechegzhanina, he took his mother's name and was adopted by Chekhonin, her second husband. He claims to have produced sketches for plates at the State Porcelain Factory through 1919 and the early '20s. Since 1928 he has been living in Paris. (See caption for plate no. 60.)

Yakimovskaya
Ekaterina Alexandrovna
1895–?
Graduated from the School for the Deaf and Dumb, St. Petersburg (1913); studied art at the Society for the Encouragement of the Arts (1915–17). In 1918 entered the art department of the State Porcelain Factory. She worked as a painter, first at the Stieglitz School premises, then at the factory itself, mainly copying, but also creating some designs of her own.

Zimin
Grigorii Dimitrievich
1875–1958
Studied the painting techniques of the Imperial glass and porcelain factories (1891–3); worked as a painter at the Imperial Porcelain Factory (1893–1919) and at the State Porcelain Factory (1922–58). In 1903, he was sent to France, Germany, Austria and Sweden to study the technique of underglaze painting. Known for his delicate brushwork and lyrical landscape painting.

1
IPF monogram for Nicholas II, 1898 in green underglaze; SPF mark of hammer, sickle and cog, 1921, plus special RSFSR monogram designed by Chekhonin, and Chekhonin's initials, all by Chekhonin in gold, green and wine-red overglaze.

2
IPF monogram for Alexander III, 1893, in green underglaze; elegantly painted SPF mark of hammer, sickle and cog in blue overglaze; 1921 and initials in black overglaze, all by Chekhonin.

3
Obliterated IPF monogram; SPF mark of hammer, sickle and cog; Maria Lebedeva's monogram of a swan resting on an M (*Lebedev* is the Russian word for swan), plus 1921, all by Lebedeva in dark-green overglaze.

4
IPF monogram for Nicholas II, 1899 in green underglaze; SPF mark of hammer, sickle and cog, 1921 in blue overglaze; 'po riz Lebedevoi' (based on drawing by Lebedeva) and initials MK (factory artist Maria Kirilova), all in dark-green overglaze.

5
SPF mark of hammer, sickle and cog in green underglaze; V. Freze's signature and 'po riz S. V. Chekhonina' (based on drawing by Chekhonin) 1926, in black overglaze.

6
IPF monogram for Nicholas II, 1909, in green underglaze; SPF mark of hammer, sickle and cog, 1922 and Z. Kobyletskaya's signature and also mark N.259/1, all in blue overglaze.

7
Provisional Government mark, 1917, in green underglaze; Sergei Chekhonin's signature in black overglaze.

8
IPF monogram for Nicholas II, 1905 in green underglaze; SPF mark of hammer, sickle and cog, 1921, and M. Adamovich's monogram, all in blue overglaze.

9
IPГ monogram for Nicholas II, 1913 in green on biscuit; SPF mark of hammer, sickle and cog, 1922; initials E. Ya. (factory artist Ekaterina Yakimovskaya) plus 'po riz Narbuta' (based on design by Narbut) and N.191/2, all in blue on biscuit.

10
SPF mark of hammer, sickle and cog, 1919 in green underglaze; 213/7 and 1922 plus MB (monogram of factory artist Maria Briantseva) in blue overglaze; impressed into the paste are the initials VL (modeller Valentin Lukhin).

11
SPF mark of hammer, sickle and cog in bright blue on biscuit; plus 'sculptor A. T. Matveev, 1926' in black on biscuit.

12
On back of the base of the copy of a Matveev figurine by Chekhonin, in latter's hand: 'Sc.A.T.Matveev, 1925, Volkhov, NGF S. Tchechonin', all in black overglaze (this is a third variation of Chekhonin's spelling of his name).

13
IPF monogram for Nicholas II, 1905 in green underglaze; SPF mark of hammer, sickle and cog, 1922, and Chekhonin's initials in Cyrillic, and full signature in Latin letters, all in wine-red overglaze.

14
VKhUTEMAS mark in iron-red overglaze.

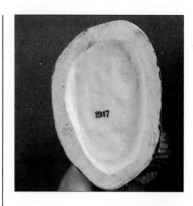

15
1917 in green overglaze (Used only during the first two months after the abdication of the Romanovs).

19
IPF monogram for Alexander III, 1889 in green underglaze; SPF mark of hammer and sickle, 1922 plus N.3/13 in blue overglaze.

16
Provisional Government mark, 1917, used between April and December 1917, in green underglaze, SPF mark of hammer, sickle and cog, 1922, plus initials E. Ya. (Ekaterina Yakimovskaya) and N.139/5, 'po riz Adamovicha' (based on a design by Adamovich), all in blue overglaze.

20
IPF monogram for Nicholas II, 1898 in green underglaze; SPF mark of hammer, sickle and cog, 1923 and 506/12 in blue overglaze.

17
Provisional Government mark obliterated with round green paint patch; SPF mark of hammer, sickle and cog, 1918 in blue overglaze.

21
IPF monogram obliterated with oval green paint patch; SPF mark of hammer, sickle and cog, 1919 in blue overglaze.

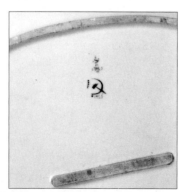

18
IPF monogram for Alexander II in green underglaze; SPF mark of hammer, sickle and cog, 1925 in blue overglaze.

22
IPF monogram obliterated with diamond-shaped green paint patch; SPF mark of hammer, sickle and cog in blue underglaze.

23
IPF monogram for Nicholas II, 1913 in green underglaze; SPF mark of hammer, sickle and cog in black overglaze, plus signature, Sergei Chekhonin, in Cyrillic, 1921, in black overglaze.

24
Novgubfarfor monogram, NGF, Volkhov, 1924, and Cyrillic signature, Sergei Checkhonin, all by Chekhonin in black overglaze.

25
Novgubfarfor monogram, NGF, Volkhov, 1924, 'based on design by Chekhonin' and initials MK (factory artist Maria Kirilova) all by Kirilova in black overglaze.

26
IPF monogram for Nicholas II, 1901 in green underglaze; SPF mark of hammer, sickle and cog and Kobyletskaya's mark, a cross within a circle, plus 1921, all in blue overglaze.

27
IPF monogram for Nicholas II, 1909 in green underglaze; SPF mark of hammer, sickle and cog, 1921 and Varvara Rukavishnikova's interlaced VR monogram, all in blue overglaze.

28
SPF mark of hammer, sickle and cog and indecipherable date in green underglaze; signature, E. Yakimovskaya, 1921 in blue overglaze.

29
Special gold famine mark designed by Chekhonin. It was painted onto 23 pieces created in 1921, to be sold in aid of the famine victims.

30
SPF mark of hammer, sickle and cog, 1924, plus Natalya and Elena Danko's joint monogram (N and E, in and under a stylized D) all in black overglaze.

31
IPF monogram for Alexander III, 1893 in green underglaze; SPF mark of hammer, sickle and cog and N.332/1 in blue overglaze plus trefoil mark of factory artist Vasilii Timorev, followed by 22.V. and 'po V.M.' (based on design by V. M. – Mosyagin) all in blue overglaze.

32
IPF monogram for Nicholas II, 1902 or 1908 (unclear) in green underglaze; special jubilee mark designed by Chekhonin for Fifth Anniversary of SPF/KNP. This black overglaze mark was placed on all articles decorated at the SPF from 23 March until 31 December 1923, in lieu of the usual SPF mark, to commemorate the fact that the SPF was placed under the authority of Narkompros five years earlier and was involved in their propaganda campaign. 'Po riz A. Shchekotikhinoi' (based on design by A. Shchekotikhina) and initials MK (for factory artist Maria Kirilova) also in black overglaze.

33
IPF monogram for Nicholas II, 1912 in green underglaze; SPF mark of hammer and sickle and initials. A.Shch. (Shchekotikhina), all in blue overglaze.

34
IPF monogram for Nicholas II, 1904 in green underglaze; SPF mark of hammer, sickle and cog, 1922 plus N.570/3 and signature of V. Shcherbakov, all in blue overglaze.

35
IPF monogram for Nicholas II, 1914 in green underglaze; SPF mark of hammer, sickle and cog, 1918 in blue overglaze; signature, G. Zimin, and 1918 in grey overglaze.

36
IPF monogram for Nicholas II, 1908 in green underglaze; SPF mark of hammer, sickle and cog, 1921 plus initials L.G. (Liubov Gaush), all in overglaze.

37
IPF monogram obliterated with diamond-shaped green paint patch: SPF mark of hammer, sickle and cog, 1920, plus initials N.G. (Natalya Girshfeld) in blue overglaze.

38
SPF mark of hammer, sickle and cog in green underglaze; signature, A. Vorobevsky, 1927, in grey overglaze.

39
IPF monogram for Nicholas II, 1898 in green underglaze; SPF mark of hammer, sickle and cog, 1923, plus N. 660/7 and 'Po riz Malevicha'. (based on drawing by Malevich) all in black overglaze.

40
IPF monogram for Nicholas II, 1904, in green underglaze; SPF mark of hammer, sickle and cog, 'Suprematism 474', plus a black square within a square, signed 'Suetin', all in Cyrillic and in black overglaze. LPF inventory letters and number, 2939.

41
IPF monogram for Nicholas II, 1904, in green underglaze; SPF mark of hammer, sickle and cog, 'Suprematism 474', a black square within a square, and signed 'Il. Chashnik,' all in Cyrillic and in black overglaze. LPF inventory letters and number, 3127.

42
IPF monogram for Nicholas II, 1911, in green underglaze; special mark for fifth anniversary of the Red Army, consisting of a hammer, sickle, cog and star, plus 1923. Also, Adamovich's signature, 'M. Adamovich', all in Cyrillic, in overglaze. LPF inventory letters and number, 26.

43
SPF mark of hammer, sickle and cog, 1923, plus N.660/21 and 'po riz Malevicha' (based on drawing by Malevich), 'Suprematism', and a black square within a square, all in black overglaze. LPF inventory letters and number, 2125.

44
SPF mark of hammer, sickle and cog, 1923, plus 'Suprematism, 474/9' and Suetin's signature twice – 'N. Suetin', printed 'Suetin' in script, all in Cyrillic and in black overglaze. LPF inventory letters and number, 2967.

Ѧ 1	Ѧ 2	ЊБ 3	ЕкБ 4	ЛБ 5	Л.Г. 6
Н.Т. 7	A 8	↟ 9	ДЕ 10	НДН 11	Е 12
МкМК 13	⊗ ЗВК. 14	M 15	✳ 16	БВ 17	В Р. 18
ВФ Р 19	Б 20	Ж 21	♁ 22	в.фр. В.Ф. 23	Б. 24
С.Ъ 25	Щ Щк 26	А.Т-Р. 27	В.Щ. 28	ЕЯ ЯЕ 29	Б. 30

I
Adamovich
Mikhail Mikhailovich
2
Balt
Alexandra A.
3
Blagovestchenskaya
Nadejda Sergeevna
4
Bolsheva
Ekaterina Nikolaevna
5
Briantseva
Maria Alexandrovna
6
Gaush
Liubov Nikolaevna
7
Girshfeld
Natalya A.
8
Golenkina
Alisa Rudolfovna
9
Gromov
A.
10
Danko
Elena Yakovlevna
(two versions)
11
Danko
Natalya Yakovlevna
(two versions)
12
Danko
Elena and Natalya
(combined monogram)
13
Kirilova
Maria Petrovna
14
Kobyletskaya
Zinaida Viktorovna
Kobyletskaya also sometimes used the cross within
the circle without her initials.

15
Lebedeva
Maria Vasilievna
16
Potapova
Elizaveta Nikodimovna
17, 18 and 19
Rukavishnikova
Varvara Feodorovna
(four versions)
20
Skvortsov
Alexei Alexeevich
21
Sudarchikov
Gavriil Mikhailovich
22
Timorev
Vasilii Porfirevich
23
Freze
Varvara Petrovna
(two versions)
24
Radonich
Bazilka Stepanovna
(G. V. Baranov and A. A. Balt
also sometimes used the 'B' as their monogram).
25
Chekhonin (Tchekhonine)
Sergei Vasilievich
27
Shchekotikhina-Pototskaya
Alexandra Vasilievna
(non-Cyrillic initials sometimes used by Shchekotikhina
during her second stay in Paris.
28
Shcherbakov
Valentin Semionovich
29
Yakimovskaya
Ekaterina Alexandrovna
(two versions)
30
Zimin
Grigorii Dimitrievich

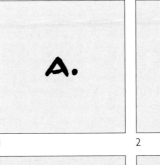
1

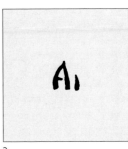
2

3

4

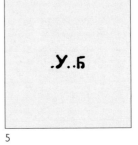
5

6

None of these monograms have been positively identified,
although no. 4 may be that of Eva Ferdinandovna **Kordes**.

Factory marks

These marks were often stamped in a rust-red colour. Nos. 1, 2, 5 and 6 invariably appear in rust red.

1   2   3   4

5   6   7   8

9   10   11   12

13   14   15   16

1
SPF and LPF export mark, 1920 onwards.
2
SPF and LPF export mark, 1923 onwards.
3
Jubilee mark, 1922, for the Fifth Anniversary of RSFSR.
4
Jubilee mark for the fifth anniversary of the SPF association with Narkompros (KNP).
5
VKhUTEMAS mark, created 1921.
6
VKhUTEMAS mark (variant) created 1921.
7
Monogram of the Novgorod Porcelain Trust and mark of the Volkhov Factory, used 1923–7.
8
Novgorod Porcelain Trust/Volkhov Factory, 1923 (variant of no.7).
9
Dimitrov Factory, first Soviet era mark, 1918–19.
10
Dimitrov Factory mark, 1920–25.
11
Dimitrov Factory trademark, 1925–30, under the Porcelain Trust.
12
Dimitrov Factory mark and trademark, 1925 and later, under Porcelain Trust.
13
Dulevo Porcelain Factory, first Soviet era mark, 1918–19.
14
Dulevo Porcelain Factory, 1920–23.
15
Dulevo Porcelain Factory, 1924–25.
16
Dulevo Porcelain Factory export mark, 1926–29.

The Symbols on Propaganda Porcelain, and their Meanings

(some are universally recognized, others are specific to the Soviet regime)

anchor	hope
books	literacy, knowledge
broken chains	emancipation
bundle of arrows or lances	union, alliance
classical columns and collapsing buildings	the past giving way
cog, or part of a cog	industry
crown of oak, oak tree, or crown of laurel leaves or tree	victory, the reward for valour and virtue
dove	peace, gentleness
ears or sheaves of wheat	riches, brought to the State by agriculture
fortress or kremlin	the invincible Soviet Republic
hammer and sickle	the union of workers and peasants
maiden in classical dress	freedom
Mercury's wand	peace
mirror	truth
plough, hoe, scythe, sickle, pitchfork, rake, plants, fruit	abundance, agriculture
Phrygian bonnet	freedom
red train advancing	the progress of the Soviet State
red star	symbol both for the Soviet State and the Red Army
cockerel	vigilance
scale	justice
the sun and its rays	emancipation
Red Army soldier slaying a dragon	the Revolution overcoming the counter-revolution
double-headed eagle, half eagle	the Romanov reign
serpent	prudence
trumpet	the hailing of the new era

Picture credits

We are grateful to the following sources for allowing us to reproduce the pictures listed (numbers refer to figure references in the book):
The Badisches Landesmuseum, Karlsruhe, 28
Christie's, London, 13, 26 and 42
The Gilman Paper Company Collection, New York, 164
The Kunstgewerbe Museum, Cologne, 165
The Lomonosov Porcelain Factory, 4, 32, 150–154, 161–163, 166–169 and 171
Manchester City Art Galleries, 96
The Russian Museum, Leningrad, 87 and 173
Sotheby's, London, 62, 157 and 170
The Stroganov School of Art and Industrial Design, Moscow, 155 and 156

Figures 15, 24, 58, 63 and 73 were loaned from a collection in London, and 7, 18, 33, 34, 39, 61, 69 and 89 from other collections in England. Other pictures loaned from private collections were 67, 68, 83 and 103, from Greece, 88, 97, 99 and 101, from Leningrad, 20 and 74, from Moscow, and 5, from Paris. All other photographs of porcelain were reproduced by kind permission of Nicholas Lynn.

The pictures of Natalya and Elena Danko on page 16 were loaned from a private collection in Leningrad. The picture of the agit train on page 27 was loaned by David King.

Bibliography

Russian Reference Books and Articles

Andreeva, L., 'O Poslednikh godakh tvorchestva S. Chekhonina', *Sovietskoe Dekorativnoe Iskusstvo '76*, Sovietskii Khudozhnik, Moscow, 1978.
– *Sovietskie Farfor 1920–1930*, Sovietskii Khudozhnik, Moscow, 1975.

Baranova, O., *Kouskovo* (the State Museum of Ceramics), Aurora Art Publishers, Leningrad, 1983.

Ephros, A., and Punin, N., *S. Chekhonin*, Moscow State Publishing House, 1923 (editions in Russian, English and French).

Gollerbach, E., *RSFSR La Porcelaine de la Manufacture d'Etat*, published under the direction of Jean Lazarevsky, Mospeschat, Moscow, 1922.

Gollerbach, E., and Farmakovski, M. (editors), *Russkie Farfor – La Porcelaine d'Art Russe*, Receuil d'Articles sur la Manufacture de Porcelaine de l'Etat, State Publishing House, Leningrad, 1924.

Lansere, A., *Sovietskie Farfor/Soviet Porcelain*, Khudozhnik RSFSR, Leningrad, 1974.

Lianda, N., 'Agitazionii Farfor S. V. Chekhonina', *Voprozi Razbitia Sovietskovo Iskusstva i Iskusstva Narodov SSSR*, Institut Zhivopisii Skulpturii i Arkhitekturii – Repin, Leningrad, 1972.

Nikiforova, L., *Russian Porcelain/Russkie Farfor in the Hermitage Collection*, Aurora Art Publishers, Leningrad, 1973.

Ovsyannikov, Y., 'Iesli bi Natalya Danko Byela Dnevnik', *Panorama Iskusstv*, No. 6, Moscow, 1983.
– *Skultor v Krasnom Khalate*, Sovietskii Khudozhnik, Moscow, 1965.

Tolstoy, V. (ed), *Sovietskie Dekorativnoe Iskusstvo Materiali & Dokumenti 1917–1932, Farfor Faians Steklo*, Iskusstvo, Moscow, 1980.

Sovietskie Farfor (booklet, cover by Chekhonin, very rare), Moskovskoe Khudozhestvennye Izdatelistvo, Moscow, 1927.

Zrelische, no. 26, Moscow, 1923.

Exhibition Catalogues

100 Years of Russian Art From Private Collections in the USSR, 1889–1989, D. Elliott and V. Dudakov (editors), Lund Humphries in association with the Barbican Art Gallery and the Museum of Modern Art, Oxford, London, 1989.

Art and Revolution 1910–1932, catalogue of an exhibition at the Seibu Museum of Art, Tokyo, 1982.

Art into Production – Soviet Textiles, Fashions and Ceramics 1917–1935, David Elliot (ed), catalogue of an exhibition at the Museum of Modern Art, Oxford, and the Crafts Council, London, 1984 and 1985.

Avanguardia Russa Dalle Collezione Private Sovietiche Origini E Percorso 1904–1934, catalogue of an exhibition of Soviet painting and porcelain at the Palazzo Reale, Milan, Edizioni Bolis, srl, Bergamo, 1989.

Kunst und Revolution/Art and Revolution, Russian and Soviet Art 1910–1932, catalogue of an exhibition at the Austrian Museum of Applied Arts, Vienna, 1988.

Moscow-Paris 1910–1930, catalogue of an exhibition at the Georges Pompidou Centre, Paris, 1979.

Porcelain and Propaganda, catalogue of an exhibition at Fischer Fine Art Ltd., London, 1978.

La Rivoluzione in salotto Porcellane Sovietiche 1917–1930, catalogue of an exhibition of Soviet porcelain in Venice, Electa, Milan, 1988.

Sovietskii Khudozhestvennye Farfor 1918–1923, B. I. Alekseev (ed) and others, catalogue of an exhibition of Soviet Porcelain at the Ceramics Museum, Kuskovo, Isdatelistvo Akademie Khudozhestv SSSR, Moscow, 1962.

Magazine and Newspaper Articles

Ades, Dawn, 'The Shock of the Old', *Crafts*, No. 71, November/December 1984.

Atterbury, Paul, 'Revolutionary Collection', *Ceramics*, February/March 1986.

Franzke, Irmela, 'Russisches Porzellan mit Suprematistischem Dekor im Badischen Landesmuseum Karlsruhe', *Keramos*, Heft 78, October, 1977.
– 'Zum Dekorationsstil russischer Porzellane im ersten Jahrzehnt nach der Oktober-Revolution', *Jahrbuch der Staatlichen Kunstsammlungen in Baden-Wurttemberg*, Band 12, Deutscher Kunstverlag, 1975.

Horwell, Veronica, 'Propaganda on a Plate', *Observer* magazine, 13 December 1987.

Lobanov-Rostovsky, Nina, 'Soviet Propaganda Porcelain', *Journal of Decorative and Propaganda Arts*, no. 11, Miami, 1989.

Paterson, Moira, 'Soviet China', *Observer* magazine, 2 December 1984.

Raeburn, Walter, 'Pottery and Propaganda', *Apollo*, January 1966.

Books, Magazines and Catalogues for General Reference

Barron, S. and Tuchman, M. (editors), *The Avant-Garde in Russia 1910–1930 New Perspectives*, catalogue of an exhibition at Los Angeles County Museum of Art, 1980.

de Boisanger, C., *Moscou en 1925, l'URSS entre Lenine et Staline*, La Pensée Universelle, Paris, 1981.

Bowlt, John, *Russian Stage Design, Scenic Innovation, 1900–1930, from the Collection of Mr. and Mrs. Nikita D. Lobanov-Rostovsky*, Mississippi Museum of Art, 1982.

– Bowlt, J. (editor), *Journey into Non-Objectivity, The Graphic Work of Kazimir Malevich and other Members of the Russian Avant-Garde*, exhibition catalogue, Dallas Museum of Fine Arts, 1980.

Elliott, David, *New Worlds: Russian Art and Society 1900–1937*, Thames and Hudson, London, 1986.

Faïences et Objets Révolutionnaires, catalogue of the P. M. Sestié collection of French revolutionary ceramics, exhibited at the Conservatoire François Joseph Gossec, Gagny, Ile de France, 1989.

Fülop-Miller, R., *The Mind and Face of Bolshevism*, first published in German in 1926, in English 1927, re-issued, Harper & Row, 1965.

Gray, Camilla, *The Great Experiment: Russian Art 1863–1922*, Harry N. Abrams, New York, 1962.

Guerman,, M., *Art of the October Revolution*, Collet's, London, 1979.

Karshan, D., *Malevich, the Graphic Work: 1913–1930*, A print catalogue raisonné, Israel Museum, Jerusalem, 1975.

Khan-Magomedov, S. O. *Alexandr Vesnin and Russian Constructivism*, Lund Humphries, London, 1986.

Lodder, C., *Russian Constructivism*, Yale University Press, New Haven, and London, 1983.

Lyons, E., *Assignment in Utopia*, Harrap, London, 1938.

Malewitsch, catalogue of an exhibition at the Galerie Gmurzynska, Cologne, 1978.

Milner, J., *Vladimir Tatlin and the Russian Avant-Garde*, Yale University Press, New Haven and London, 1983.

Nakov, A. and Nussberg, L. (editors), *Ilya G. Tschaschnik*, catalogue of an exhibition at the Kunstmuseum, Dusseldorf/Bauhaus Archiv, Berlin, 1978.

Ransome, A., *Six Weeks in Russia in 1919*, George Allen & Unwin, London, 1919.

Reed, John, *Ten Days that Shook the World*, first published in 1919, Penguin Books, London, 1986.

Rudenstine, A. (editor), *Russian Avant-Garde Art, the George Costakis Collection*, Harry N. Abrams, New York, 1981.

Russische Avant-Garde, 1910–1930, catalogue of the Ludwig Collection, Ludwig Museum, Cologne, Prestel Verlag, Munich, 1986.

Salisbury, Harrison E., *Russia in Revolution 1900–1930*, Andre Deutsch, London, 1978.

Shukman, Harold (editor), *The Blackwell Encyclopaedia of the Russian Revolution*, Basil Blackwell, Oxford, 1989.

Shadowa, L., *Suche und Experiment, Russische und Sowjetische Kunst 1910 bis 1930*, VEB Verlag der Kunst, Dresden, 1978.

White, S., *The Bolshevik Poster*, Yale University Press, New Haven and London, 1988.

Williams, R., *Artists in Revolution: Portraits of the Russian Avant-Garde 1905–1925*, Indiana University Press, 1977.

Index

(Figures in italics refer to captions to illustrations)